MW01193151

Best Easy Day Hikes
Missouri Ozarks

Help Us Keep This Guide Up to Date

Every effort has been made by the authors and editors to make this guide as accurate and useful as possible. However, many things can change after a guide is published—trails are rerouted, regulations change, facilities come under new management, etc.

We would appreciate hearing from you concerning your experiences with this guide and how you feel it could be improved and kept up to date. While we may not be able to respond to all comments and suggestions, we'll take them to heart and we'll also make certain to share them with the authors. Please send your comments and suggestions to the following address:

GPP
Reader Response/Editorial Department
P.O. Box 480
Guilford, CT 06437

Or you may e-mail us at:

editorial@GlobePequot.com

Thanks for your input, and happy trails!

Best Easy Day Hikes Series

Best Easy Day Hikes
Missouri Ozarks

JD Tanner and Emily Ressler-Tanner

FALCON GUIDES

GUILFORD, CONNECTICUT
HELENA, MONTANA

FALCONGUIDES®

Copyright © 2012 Rowman & Littlefield

ALL RIGHTS RESERVED. No part of this book may be reproduced or transmitted in any form by any means, electronic or mechanical, including photocopying and recording, or by any information storage and retrieval system, except as may be expressly permitted in writing from the publisher.

FalconGuides is an imprint of Globe Pequot Press.
Falcon, FalconGuides, and Outfit Your Mind are registered trademarks of Rowman & Littlefield.

Text design: Sheryl P. Kober
Project editor: Heather Santiago
Layout: Joanna Beyer
Maps by Alena Pearce © Rowman & Littlefield

TOPO! Explorer software and SuperQuad source maps courtesy of National Geographic Maps. For information about TOPO! Explorer, TOPO!, and Nat Geo Maps products, go to www.topo.com or www.nat geomaps.com.

Library of Congress Cataloging-in-Publication Data is available on file.

ISBN 978-0-7627-7791-4

Printed in the United States of America

Distributed by NATIONAL BOOK NETWORK

The authors and Rowman & Littlefield assume no liability for accidents happening to, or injuries sustained by, readers who engage in the activities described in this book.

Contents

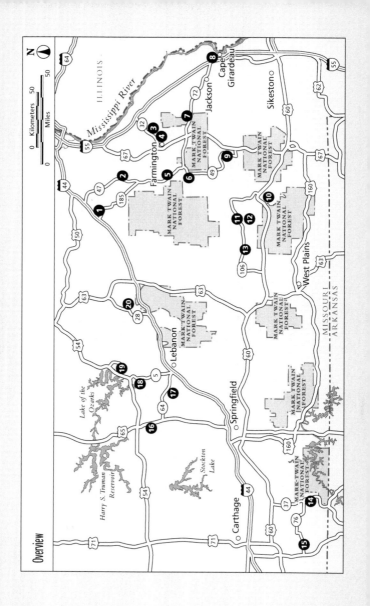

Overview

Acknowledgments

We would like to send out a special thank-you to all the land managers who patiently answered our questions, pointed us toward the very best trails, and carefully reviewed the trail descriptions for this guide. We would also like to thank our friends and family for accompanying us on many of the trails in the Ozarks; your company, humor, support, and enthusiasm were very much appreciated. Finally we would like to thank all of our friends at Falcon Guides, particularly Katie Benoit, Max Phelps, Jessica Haberman, and Julie Marsh, for their support and encouragement and for making a book out of our rough manuscript.

Introduction

The Ozarks is a region that offers endless beauty and solitude for outdoor enthusiasts. Hikes across long ridgetops, into quiet valleys and cool hollows, and through rocky creeks give visitors a chance to view the impressive natural history of the area. Springs, caves, sinkholes, bluffs, glades, hardwood forests, clear-flowing streams, waterfalls, and lakes are the natural gems of the Ozarks, and all are highlighted in this guide.

The Ozarks are a vast region, covering over 60,000 square-acres and spreading across Arkansas, Missouri, Oklahoma, and Kansas. Some argue that the region also includes southern Illinois. While the boundaries of the Ozarks are somewhat muddled, the name of the region itself is even more confusing. Depending on who is describing the area, you may hear the region referred to as the Ozark Mountains, the Ozark Highlands, the Ozark Upland, the Ozark Hills, the Ozark Hill Country, the Ozark Plateau, or the Ozarks. Given the large geographical area, the diversity of scenery, the sporadic pockets of populated areas, and the unique vernacular of those who live here, it is easy to see how labeling the area with just one name has been a challenge.

Once a large plateau, the Ozarks are not particularly high in elevation. The most mountainlike areas include the St. Francois Mountains in Missouri and the Boston and Ouachita Mountains in Arkansas. The region is characterized by a wealth of springs, caves, and sinkholes and owes its unique characteristics to the power of erosion. Over time water has changed the plateau, carving away portions of the soil and the underlying sedimentary rocks and leaving the hills, valleys, exposed bluffs, and fascinating rock formations we see today.

This guide lists easy, moderate, and more challenging hikes in the Missouri Ozarks. Some of the hikes can be found near more-populated areas such as St. Louis, Cape Girardeau, and Springfield. Most are nestled in the heart of the Missouri Ozarks and may require a bit of driving to find the trailhead. All showcase the region's natural wonders. From the highest elevation in Missouri to one of the largest springs in the country, the hikes featured in this guide are twenty of the best easy day hikes in the region. We have done our best to include a little of something for everyone. Hikes for families, for birding, for scenic views, for history buffs, and for pets have all been included and should be considered an introduction to the areas and a starting point to continue your explorations.

The Nature of the Ozarks

Ozark area trails range from rugged and hilly to flat and paved. Hikes in this guide cover a little bit of everything. While by definition a best easy day hike is not strenuous and poses little danger to the traveler, knowing a few details about the nature of the Ozarks will enhance your explorations.

Weather

The weather in the Ozarks consists of a mild spring, ranging from cool to warm and muggy and is typically wet. Trail conditions can be quite muddy during spring, especially for hikes that are in or near floodplains. The biggest concern for spring weather in the Ozarks is the chance for thunder/lightning storms, hail, and/or tornadoes.

Storms still pose a threat in early summer, but as the summer progresses the weather tends to be less wet and sometimes very hot and almost always humid. Hikers that choose to get out in the mid- to late-summer might consider early-morning hikes, as high temperatures and humidity usually set in by midmorning.

Fall can be downright gorgeous in the Ozarks. The mostly hardwood forests often exhibit a dazzling array of fall colors. Daytime temperatures in the low to mid-70s along with decreased humidity make for some amazingly scenic hikes. Fall hiking cannot be encouraged enough.

The Ozarks have an abundance of cold and snowy days in winter, but if you don't mind hiking with no leaves on the trees, winter can be a very enjoyable time to hike here as well. Wintertime hikers will get more views of the rolling hills. The unusual rock formations are made even more magical after a light dusting of snow, and hikers will typically enjoy the trails almost all to themselves.

Ideal times for hiking in the Ozarks are early to late spring and mid to late fall. Mix in the handful of cool days in summer and warm winter days and a person can enjoy many picture-perfect hiking days in the Ozarks each year.

Hazards

There are a few hazards to be aware of and to prepare for when hiking in the Ozarks. Poison ivy, a year-round hazard, might be the most common and most annoying issue hikers will come across while hiking here. Poison ivy has been found in every county in Missouri, and it is estimated that somewhere between 50 and 70 percent of people experience a physical reaction after coming in contact with the plant. Poison ivy can grow as a woody shrub up to 6 feet high or as a vine that clings to other trees and shrubs. While the old expression "Leaves of three, let it be" is good advice to follow, several other three-leaf plants grow in the Ozarks, so be sure to educate yourself about poison ivy before hitting the trail. Poison ivy can be found on almost every hike in this book.

Ticks are most abundant in the region during spring and summer. There are many different types of ticks, but the two most common in Missouri are the Lone Star tick and the American dog tick. Ticks have been known to carry, and occasionally spread, the organisms that cause Lyme disease, Rocky Mountain spotted fever, and tularemia. Ticks are unavoidable but are no reason to avoid hiking in spring and summer. Hikers should wear lighter colored clothing to help detect ticks, use repellent that is proven effective against ticks, periodically check for ticks during your hike, and perform a complete body check on yourself and your pet after every hike. During spring and summer, ticks can be found on every hike in this book.

There are fifty different species of mosquitoes in Missouri, and the most common concern with mosquitoes is the West Nile virus. It is estimated that only 1 percent of mosquitoes carry West Nile virus, and only 1 percent of people bitten will actually contract the virus. Like ticks, mosquitoes should not be a reason to avoid hiking in spring or summer. Simply be aware and be prepared. To help you avoid mosquitoes, use insect repellent, wear long pants and long-sleeve shirts, avoid hiking at dawn or dusk, and don't wear perfume or cologne when hiking. Mosquitoes can be found on every hike in this book.

Venomous snakes are the fourth hazard hikers might encounter on the hikes in this book. Most of the snakes in the Ozarks are harmless; however, hikers should be aware that several species of venomous snakes do inhabit the area. Your chances of being bitten by a venomous snake in the United States are very, very low. Fewer than 8,000 people are bitten every year by a venomous snake, most while trying to handle or kill the snake, and fewer than five of those people die.

Missouri is home to five species of venomous snakes. The Osage copperhead, western cottonmouth (water moccasin), timber rattlesnake, eastern Massasauga rattlesnake (swamp rattler), and western pygmy rattlesnake (ground rattler) can all be found in or near the Ozarks. The Osage copperhead and timber rattlesnake are the venomous snakes a hiker is most likely to encounter. Venomous snakes are most commonly recognized by their "arrow-shaped" heads. Three of the five venomous snakes in Missouri are rattlesnakes and can be easily identified by the rattling noise they make when they feel threatened. To avoid being bitten, hikers should wear protective footwear, never place hands under rocks or logs, keep an eye on the ground as they hike, and never attempt to handle or kill snakes.

Other hazards you may encounter include (but are not limited to) steep drop-offs along bluffs, thunder/lightening storms, tornadoes, a growing population of black bears, and heat-related illnesses. As mentioned earlier, many of the hikes in this guide are in rural areas. Having a full tank of gas and being aware of the nearest medical facility are highly recommended.

Be Prepared

"Be prepared." The Boy Scouts say it, the Leave No Trace organization says it, and the best outdoors people say it.

Being prepared won't completely keep you out of harm's way when outdoors, but it will minimize the chances of finding yourself there. Here are some things to consider:

- Familiarize yourself with the basics of first aid (bites, stings, sprains, and breaks), carry a first-aid kit, and know how to use it.
- Hydrate! No matter where or when you are hiking, you should always carry water with you. A standard is two liters per person per day.
- Be prepared to treat water on longer hikes. It is not safe to drink directly from rivers and streams in the Ozarks. Iodine tablets are small, light, and easy to carry.
- Carry a backpack in order to store the Ten Essentials: map, compass, sunglasses/sunscreen, extra food and water, extra clothes, headlamp/flashlight, first-aid kit, fire starter, matches, and knife.
- Pack your cell phone (on vibrate) as a safety back up.
- Keep an eye on the kids. Have them carry a whistle to help you locate them, just in case they wander off.
- Bring a leash, plastic bags for dog waste, and extra water for your pets.

Leave No Trace

This hiking guide will take you to historical sites, conservation areas, national natural landmarks, and many other places of natural and cultural significance. For that reason, the importance of following the principles of Leave No Trace cannot be stressed enough.

Do your best to stick to trails to avoid inadvertently trampling sensitive vegetation. Be prepared to pack out any trash you bring with you, and remember, it never hurts to carry out trash that others have left behind. Be extra careful when visiting sites of historical and natural importance. Leave everything as you found it, and never remove artifacts from these sensitive areas.

Consider your impact on wildlife living in the environment in which you hike, and be sure not to feed wild animals, as this act is unhealthy for wildlife and dangerous for people. Respect other visitors and trail users by keeping your pets on a leash, stepping to the side of the trail to allow others to pass, and keeping noise to a minimum.

For more information on enjoying the outdoors responsibly, visit the Leave No Trace Center for Outdoor Ethics website at www.LNT.org.

Land Management

The following agencies manage the public lands where the hikes in this book are located. Contact them with any questions and concerns before visiting or while planning your visit:

Missouri Department of Natural Resources, P.O. Box 176, Jefferson City 65102; (573) 751-3443 or (800) 361-4827; www.dnr.mo.gov

Missouri Department of Conservation, Headquarters, 2901 West Truman Blvd., Jefferson City 65109; (573) 522-4115; http://mdc.mo.gov

Missouri Department of Natural Resources, Division of State Parks, P.O. Box 176, Jefferson City, MO 65102; (800) 361-4827 or (573) 751-3443; http://mostateparks .com

National Park Service, www.nps.gov

Keep in mind that from the time this book was published to the time that you are reading it, some land management rules and regulations may already have changed. Always check for new and updated information about the area you plan to visit.

How to Use This Guide

This guide is designed to be simple and easy to use. Each hike is described with a map and summary information that delivers the trail's vital statistics including length, difficulty, fees and permits, park hours, canine compatibility, and trail contacts. Directions to the trailhead are also provided, along with a general description of what you'll see along the way. A detailed route finder (Miles and Directions) sets forth mileages between significant landmarks along the trail.

How the Hikes Were Chosen

This guide describes trails that are accessible to every hiker visiting the Missouri Ozarks. They range in difficulty from flat excursions perfect for a family outing to more challenging treks in the rolling hills of the Ozarks. While these trails are among the best, keep in mind that nearby trails, sometimes in the same park or in a neighboring open space, may offer options better suited to your needs.

Selecting a Hike

These are all easy hikes, but easy is a relative term. Some would argue that no hike involving any kind of climbing is easy, but climbs are a fact of life in the Ozarks.

Easy hikes are generally short and flat, taking no longer than an hour to complete.

Moderate hikes involve increased distance and relatively mild changes in elevation and will take one to two hours to complete.

More challenging hikes feature some steep stretches, greater distances and generally take longer than two hours to complete.

Keep in mind that what you think is easy is entirely dependent on your level of fitness and the adequacy of your gear (primarily shoes). Use the trail's length as a gauge of its relative difficulty—even if climbing is involved, it won't be too strenuous if the hike is less than 1 mile long. The Trail Finder lists Best Long Hikes, which are more challenging than others due to length and elevation changes. If you are hiking with a group, select a hike that's appropriate for the least fit and prepared in your party.

Hiking times are based on the assumption that on flat ground, most walkers average 2 miles per hour. Adjust that rate by the steepness of the terrain and your level of fitness (subtract time if you're an aerobic animal and add time if you're hiking with kids), and you have a ballpark hiking duration. Be sure to add more time if you plan to picnic or take part in other activities like birding or photography.

Trail Finder

Best Hikes for Birders

Best Hikes with Children

Best Hikes with Dogs

Best Hikes for Great Views

Best Hikes for Nature Lovers

Best Hikes for History Buffs

Map Legend

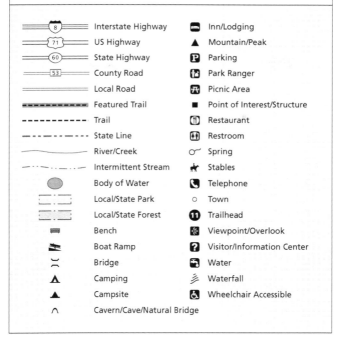

8 Interstate Highway		Inn/Lodging
71 US Highway	▲	Mountain/Peak
60 State Highway	🅿	Parking
53 County Road		Park Ranger
Local Road		Picnic Area
Featured Trail	■	Point of Interest/Structure
Trail		Restaurant
State Line		Restroom
River/Creek	☞	Spring
Intermittent Stream	★	Stables
Body of Water		Telephone
Local/State Park	○	Town
Local/State Forest	**11**	Trailhead
Bench		Viewpoint/Overlook
Boat Ramp	**?**	Visitor/Information Center
Bridge		Water
▲ Camping	⋙	Waterfall
▲ Campsite		Wheelchair Accessible
⌒ Cavern/Cave/Natural Bridge		

1 Meramec State Park: Wilderness Trail

The Wilderness Trail in Meramec State Park is a beautiful hike through a portion of the park's 6,896 acres. While the park offers several miles of hiking/backpacking trails and numerous backcountry camping sites, the caves tend to be the park's biggest draw. More than forty caves grace the area, including the popular Fisher Cave.

Distance: 8.6-mile lollipop
Hiking time: 5 hours
Difficulty: More challenging due to length
Best season: Spring through fall
Other trail users: None
Canine compatibility: Leashed dogs permitted
Fees and permits: No fees or permits required

Maps: USGS Meramec State Park; trail map available at the park office
Trail contacts: Meramec State Park, 115 Meramec Park Dr., Sullivan 63080; (573) 468-6072; www.mostateparks.com/meramec.htm
Special considerations: Ticks and mosquitoes are common during warmer months.

Finding the trailhead: From Sullivan take MO 185 south and drive 2.6 miles to the park entrance on the right (west). Follow Meramec Drive for 0.3 mile and turn left (east) at the stop sign. After 1 mile turn left (north) into the parking area for the Wilderness Trail. GPS: N38 12.766' / W91 5.609'

The Hike

Located on the northern perimeter of the Ozarks, the 6,896-acre Meramec State Park is one of Missouri's natural treasures. Flanked on the east side by the Meramec River, this area is known for rich glades, mature hardwood forests, and numerous caves. Wildlife is abundant in the park, and you may encounter bobcat, white-tailed deer, and even black bear. Some of the caves are open to exploration, and you may encounter rare species of bats in some of these caves.

The Wilderness Trail is the longest trail in the park and the only trail designated for backpacking. Eight backpacking camps are provided along the trail, although hikers looking for a more challenging day hike can hike it in a single day. The Wilderness Trail cuts through the most rugged and remote areas of the park. From the Meramec Upland Forest Natural Area to Copper Hollow and Copper Hollow Spring, this area teems with diversity, and new sights seem to appear around every bend in the trail.

From the parking area and trailhead, begin hiking north on the Wilderness Trail. At 0.2 mile you reach the trail register; sign in and continue hiking west. You reach the loop portion of the trail at 0.4 mile. Bear left (northwest) and pass the first two backcountry campsites at 0.6 and 0.7 mile. Pass the trail access to the campsites and make your way into and out of Campbell Hollow before reaching and crossing MO 185 Spur at 2.0 miles.

Continue hiking north and pass a white-blazed connector trail on the right at 2.4 miles before you reach a series of backcountry campsites at Miles 2.5, 3.3, 3.4, and 3.7. After the last backcountry campsite the trail begins a steep descent into Copper Hollow. As the hollow opens up at 4.3 miles, you come to Copper Hollow Spring. From the spring continue hiking east to catch a quick glimpse of the Meramec River before the trail turns west.

At 6.2 miles you reach the white-blazed connector trail again and then cross MO 185 Spur again at 6.8 miles. Hike

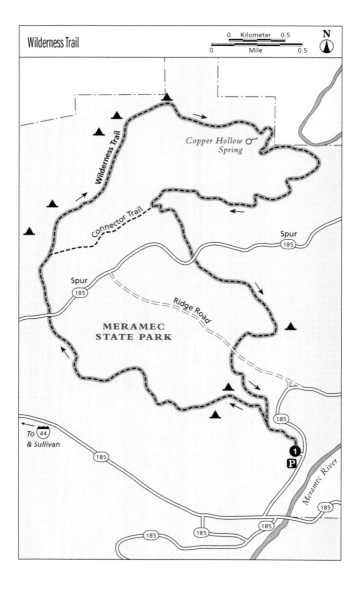

Wilderness Trail

0 Kilometer 0.5
0 Mile 0.5

N

Copper Hollow ♂ Spring

Wilderness Trail

Connector Trail

Spur 185

Spur 185

Ridge Road

MERAMEC STATE PARK

To 44 & Sullivan

185

185

185   185   185

185

1
P

Meramec River

southeast after crossing the road toward the last backcountry campsite at 7.4 miles, and then cross Ridge Road (a service road) at 7.7 miles. The trail continues south and then southeast to the end of the loop at 8.2 miles. Return to the trailhead and parking area at 8.6 miles.

Miles and Directions

0.0   Start at the Wilderness Trail parking area and trailhead, and begin hiking north.

0.2   Sign in at the trail register.

0.4   Loop portion of the trail begins; stay left (northwest).

0.6   Trail to the right leads to a backcountry campsite.

0.7   Trail to the left leads to a backcountry campsite.

2.0   The trail crosses MO 185 Spur; continue north.

2.4   A connector trail enters from the right.

2.5   Trails to the left (west) go to backcountry campsites.

3.3   Trails to the left lead to backcountry campsites at 3.3, 3.4, and 3.7 miles.

4.3   Reach Copper Hollow Spring.

6.2   A connector trail comes in from the right (west).

6.8   Trail crosses MO 185 Spur; continue southeast.

7.4   Trail to the left (east) leads to the last backcountry campsite.

7.7   Trail crosses Ridge Road; continue south.

8.2   Reach the end of the loop; turn left to return to the trailhead.

8.6   Arrive back at the trailhead and parking.

2 Washington State Park: Rockywood Trail

Washington State Park contains the largest known collection of petroglyphs in Missouri. In addition to the 1,000-year-old rock carvings, the park also offers rugged Ozark terrain to hiking enthusiasts. The Rockywood Trail is the park's longest trail.

Distance: 6.3-mile loop
Hiking time: About 3 hours
Difficulty: Moderate due to the length of the trail
Best season: Any
Other trail users: None
Canine compatibility: Leashed dogs permitted
Fees and permits: No fees or permits required

Maps: USGS Tiff; trail map available at the Thunderbird Lodge
Trail contacts: Washington State Park, 13041 MO 104, DeSoto 63020; (636) 586-2995; http://mostateparks.com/washington.htm
Special considerations: Use caution when crossing park roads. Ticks are common during warmer months.

Finding the trailhead: From DeSoto, MO, drive south for 8.1 miles on MO 21 and turn right onto MO 104 East. Enter Washington State Park and continue 1.1 miles to Thunderbird Lodge parking area and Rockywood Trail trailhead. GPS: N38 5.126' / W90 41.061'

The Hike

Located near DeSoto, Missouri, Washington State Park has a rich cultural and natural history. Several Native American rock carvings, or petroglyphs, have been found in the park, and unlike many of the rock carving found in this part of the country, they have largely escaped vandalism. People of the Middle Mississippi Culture are thought to have made the petroglyphs around AD 1000.

The Rockywood Trail is the longest and most rugged trail in the park and is designed for both hiking and backpacking. Highlights of the trail include beautiful open glades, rugged hardwood woodlands, and several scenic overlooks. A short detour from the trail will take you to one of the park's most popular interpretive areas, which contains more than a dozen petroglyphs carved into slabs of limestone.

From the Thunderbird Lodge parking lot, locate the trailhead on the west side of the lodge. Begin hiking northwest behind the Thunderbird Lodge to a set of stairs leading up the bluff. The trail crosses Dugout Road at 0.5 mile and then reaches a trail junction at 0.8 mile. Continue straight (west); the trail to the left (south) is the Opossum Track Trail. At 2.2 miles the trail makes a sharp right and continues south.

As you hike east along the trail, you will cross MO 104 at 4.3 miles and again at 5.7 miles. The Rockywood Trail joins the 1,000 Steps Trail at 5.8 miles, where you will turn left (west) to continue down the 1,000 steps. When you reach the bottom of the steps at 6.1 miles, turn left (west) and continue on to the east side of the parking area and end of the Rockywood Trail at 6.3 miles.

Miles and Directions

0.0   Start at the trailhead to the left of Thunderbird Lodge and turn right (northwest) onto the Rockywood Trail.

0.5   Cross Dugout Road and continue hiking west.

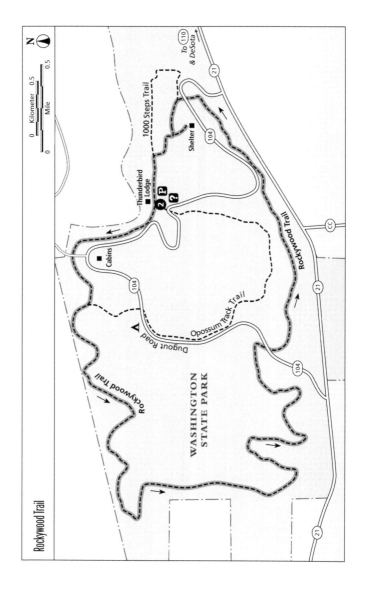

0.8 Continue straight (west) on the Rockywood Trail. The Opossum Track Trail splits to the left (south).

2.2 The trail turns to the right (south).

4.3 Trail crosses MO 104; continue south.

5.7 The trail crosses MO 104 again; continue north.

5.8 Turn left (west) and descend the 1,000 Steps Trail.

6.1 Turn left (west) at the bottom of the 1,000 steps.

6.3 Arrive back at the parking area.

3 Hawn State Park: Whispering Pines Trail–North Loop

Looping through a mixed hardwood and pine forest, the north loop of the Whispering Pines Trail offers a longer day trip for hikers wanting to take in many of the sites in Hawn State Park.

Distance: 6.5-mile loop
Hiking time: About 4 hours
Difficulty: More challenging due to length and some challenging climbs
Best season: Fall through spring
Other trail users: None
Canine compatibility: Leashed dogs permitted
Fees and permits: No fees or permits required

Maps: USGS Coffman; trail maps available at the visitor center
Trail contacts: Hawn State Park, 12096 Park Dr., Saint Genevieve 63670; (573) 883-3603; www .mostateparks.com/hawn.htm; e-mail: moparks@dnr.mo.gov
Special considerations: Ticks and poison ivy are common in warmer months.

Finding the trailhead: From Saint Genevieve drive west on MO 32 for 15.8 miles to the MO 144 junction. Turn left (east) onto MO 144 and follow the road for 2.9 miles to the park entrance. At the stop sign turn left (north) onto Park Drive and continue 1.1 miles to a fork. Stay right (south) at the fork and drive 0.1 mile to the parking area and trailhead on the left (east). GPS: N37 49.760' / W90 13.81'

The Hike

Many visitors to Hawn State Park consider it to be the loveliest park in Missouri. The 4,953-acre park is located in the eastern Ozark Mountains and is home to the 2,880-acre Whispering Pines Wild Area and Pickle Creek, a state natural area. The park was acquired by the state in 1955.

The area is believed to have been part of a large, sandy floodplain around 600 million years ago that stretched as far north as Canada. Through cycles of uplift and erosion, the sandstone cliffs and bluffs are what remain. Today hikers can enjoy rich shortleaf pine forests, mixed oak and maple trees, and plenty of flowering dogwoods. The park is also popular with rock hounds and birders.

On a windy day hikers will understand why the trail is called the Whispering Pines Trail. Many people say it sounds like the pine trees are actually whispering to you as the wind blows through them. For an extended hike or even a short, overnight backpack trip, the North Loop can be combined with the South Loop for a 10-mile hike.

From the parking area locate the Whispering Pines Trail to the south. A sign marks the trailhead, and hikers are encouraged to sign in at the trailhead register. Cross the wooden footbridge and continue hiking south to cross a second wooden footbridge at 0.1 mile. Turn right here and follow the red directional arrow southwest. At 0.3 mile come to a fork in the trail; stay right (southwest) to stay on the Whispering Pines Trail–North Loop. Wade across the babbling Pickle Creek at 1.0 mile and turn left (west). At 1.3 miles come to Connector Trail #1, which connects to the White Oaks Trail; stay left and continue hiking southwest on the North Loop. At 1.8 miles come to Connector Trail #2, which also connects to the White Oaks Trail; stay left and continue southwest.

At 3.2 miles come to Connector Trail #3 on the left (north) side of the trail, which leads to a primitive camping

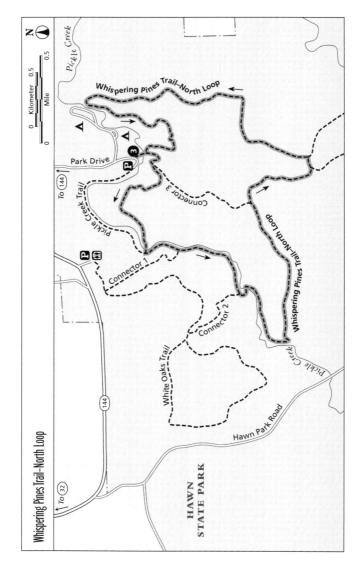

Whispering Pines Trail–North Loop

area and can be used to shorten this hike, as it eventually leads to the trailhead parking area. Stay right (east) to continue on the North Loop. At 3.7 miles come to the junction of the North and South Loops. Stay to the left (northeast) to continue on the North Loop. After 0.1 mile reach a second junction with the South Loop; again stay left (north) to continue on the North Loop and return to the trailhead. Reach Pickle Creek at 5.4 miles; follow the trail as it turns to the left (southwest). At 6.4 miles return to the footbridge; turn right (north) to cross the bridge and return to the trailhead parking area.

Miles and Directions

0.0   Start at the trailhead and bear right (south), crossing a wooden footbridge.

0.1   Cross a second wooden footbridge and turn right (southwest).

0.3   Come to a fork in the trail; stay right and continue southwest.

1.0   Cross Pickle Creek; turn left (west).

1.3   Pass Connector Trail #1.

1.8   Pass Connector Trail #2.

3.2   Pass Connector Trail #3 and continue east.

3.7   Pass the Whispering Pines Trail—South Loop and continue northeast.

3.8   Stay left (north) at the second junction with the Whispering Pines Trail—South Loop.

5.4   Come to Pickle Creek; the trail turns to the left (southwest).

6.4   Return to the wooden footbridges; turn right (north) to cross both bridges and return to the trailhead parking area.

6.5   Arrive back at the trailhead.

4 Pickle Springs Natural Area: Trail through Time

A highlight of the Pickle Springs Natural Area, this short interpretive hike features towering limestone bluffs, breezy canyons, and several interesting rock formations.

Distance: 2.0-mile loop
Hiking time: About 1 to 2 hours
Difficulty: Moderate due to modest climb
Best season: Year-round
Other trail users: None
Canine compatibility: Leashed dogs permitted
Fees and permits: No fees or permits required

Maps: USGS Sprott; interpretive trail guide available at the information kiosk
Trail contacts: Pickle Springs Natural Area, 2302 County Park Dr., Cape Girardeau 63701; (573) 290-5730
Special considerations: Use caution near bluffs. Ticks and poison ivy are common in warmer months.

Finding the trailhead: From Saint Genevieve drive west on MO 32 for 20.9 miles to State Road MO AA. Turn left (southeast) onto State Road MO AA and drive 1 mile to Dorlac Road. Turn left (north) and follow Dorlac Road for 0.5 mile along the gravel road to the parking lot and the trailhead located on the right (east). GPS: N37 48.083' / W90 18.087'

The Hike

Pickle Springs Natural Area was named for William Pickles, an Illionian who settled here in the 1850s. As more has been learned about the area, it has received more recognition.

Designated a National Natural Landmark in 1974, Pickle Springs is also a state natural area.

Researchers believe that mammoths once roamed the canyons here, grazing on plants like northern white violets, orchids, and cinnamon ferns. All these plants can still be found in Pickle Springs Natural Area, but it's the geology that keeps visitors coming back, and the Trail through Time highlights some of the areas most unusual rock formations. The LaMotte sandstone has made its way from the bottom of ancient seas to expose rock formations not typically seen in Missouri.

The Trail through Time is a 2.0-mile loop hike. The interpretive trail has been designed to lead hikers through all the area's amazing sites. Hikers will have the opportunity to enjoy beautiful rock formations, cool box canyons, and a lush forest. Some visitors will find that the hike takes longer than an hour because of all the sights.

From the parking area, begin hiking east on the obvious and well-maintained mulch trail. At 0.1 mile come to the information kiosk, which is stocked with trail maps and an interpretive pamphlet that corresponds with many of the sites along the trail. The loop begins at the kiosk; turn left (north) to continue on the one-way trail.

At 0.2 mile come to "The Slot"; turn right (east) and cross through the tight walls of LaMotte sandstone. Reach the rock formations known as Cauliflower Rocks and Double Arch at 0.4 mile. At 0.6 mile come to a wooden footbridge and continue northeast across Pickle Creek. Reach the bluff shelter known as Spirit Canyon at 1.0 mile; follow the trail as it curves to the right (west).

Cross Pickle Creek again at 1.5 miles and continue west. At 1.7 miles come to Piney Glade, a sandstone glade, near the top of the ridge and follow the trail as it curves to the

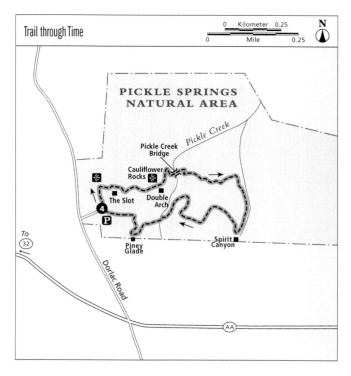

northwest. At 1.9 miles return to the information kiosk; turn left (west) and return to the parking area.

Miles and Directions

0.0   Start hiking east on the obvious mulch trail.

0.1   Come to the information kiosk; turn left (north).

0.2   Pass through The Slot.

0.4   Pass by Cauliflower Rocks and through Double Arch.

0.6   Cross Pickle Creek and continue northeast.

1.0   Reach Spirit Canyon and begin heading west.

1.5 Cross Pickle Creek and continue west.

1.7 Come to Piney Glade; follow the trail as it curves to the northeast.

1.9 Return to the information kiosk; turn left (west).

2.0 Arrive back at the trailhead parking area.

Elephant Rocks State Park: Braille Trail

Located near two of Missouri's popular state parks, Taum Sauk Mountain and Johnson's Shut-ins, Elephant Rocks State Park offers a beautiful setting. Whether you are stopping with the family for a short hike or looking for a great picnic spot to enjoy lunch between hikes at the numerous other parks in the area, Elephant Rocks State Park has plenty to offer.

Distance: 1.1-mile loop
Hiking time: About 1 hour
Difficulty: Easy due to paved trail
Best season: Fall through spring
Other trail users: None
Canine compatibility: Leashed dogs permitted
Fees and permits: No fees or permits

Schedule: Park open Apr through Oct, 8 a.m. to 8 p.m.; Nov through Mar, 8 a.m. to 5 p.m.
Fees and permits: No fees or permits required
Maps: USGS Farmington; trail map available at trailhead
Trail contacts: Missouri State Parks, 7406 MO 21, Belleview 63623; (573) 546-3454; http://mostateparks.com/park/elephant-rocks-state-park

Finding the trailhead: From Ironton drive north on MO 21 for 4.3 miles. Turn left (west) to stay on MO 21. Drive 1.6 miles on MO 21 north and turn right (north) into the Elephant Rocks State Park entrance and parking area. GPS: N37 39.183' / W90 41.34'

The Hike

Elephant Rocks State Park is a small park with plenty to see. The park sits right along MO 21 and is a popular picnicking area for travelers passing through the scenic Missouri Ozarks. The park is popular because of the 1.5-billion-year-old boulders that are lined up like a train of circus elephants. The largest of the elephant rocks has even been named Dumbo, which is estimated to tip the scales at a hefty 680 tons. Many families that visit the park take classic photos of one another pretending to push the large granite boulders. Some park visitors take advantage of its numerous picnicking sites and well-maintained playgrounds, while others apply for permits in order to climb and boulder on the huge slabs of granite in the park.

History buffs visit Elephant Rocks State Park because of its rich history as a major supplier of granite to cities throughout the state. Buildings and streets in St. Louis, Missouri, benefited from the thousands of granite blocks that were removed from the state park and the surrounding area. Graniteville, Missouri, was built right next to the park out of the stones retrieved from the quarries, and some of the buildings still sit there today. The men who worked in the quarries could earn up to $4 a day by removing chunks of granite and then sculpting them into requested sizes. Hikers looking for historical components can view an old quarry, the Engine House ruins, and rocks with holes drilled in them that were never blown apart as intended.

Elephant Rocks State Park and the 7-acre Elephant Rocks Natural Area can be enjoyed on the 1.1-mile Braille Trail. The Braille Trail uses Braille interpretive signs that allow people with visual impairments to enjoy what is in front of them. The Braille Trail is the first of its kind in Missouri state parks and is an amazing addition to what the park already has to offer.

The trailhead is located at the northern end of the parking area; take a few moments to read about the history of the area.

Begin hiking north on the well-signed and paved Braille Trail. After hiking just 0.1 mile, you reach the loop portion of the trail. Turn right (east) to begin the loop and to take full advantage of the interpretive signs, which are intended to be read while traveling counterclockwise. Continue hiking on the paved trail through a typical Missouri hardwood forest that is full of hickory and oak trees.

At 0.4 mile the trail makes a sharp left turn that sends hikers west toward the area's scenic views. A trail branching off to the right (north) leads to the Engine House ruins if you'd like to take a short detour.

After 0.5 mile reach a spur trail on the left (south) that leads to the scenic viewing area, where hikers can get up close to the Elephant Rocks. Return to the main trail via the spur trail and continue hiking west.

Come to the quarry overlook at 0.8 mile. Hike south for a short period before turning east and reaching the end of the loop at 1.0 mile. Turn right (south) to return to the trailhead at 1.1 miles.

Miles and Directions

- **0.0** Start at the trailhead and begin hiking north on the paved trail.
- **0.1** Come to the beginning of the loop; turn right (east) to hike the loop in a counterclockwise direction.

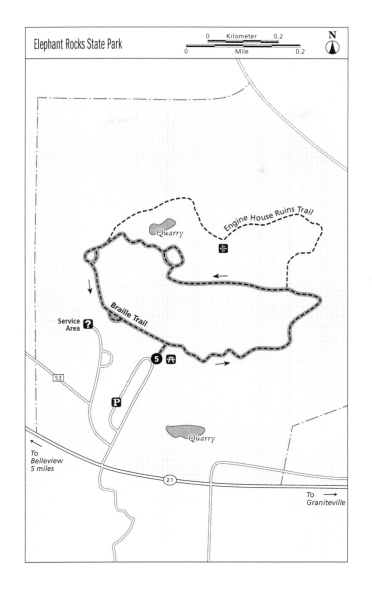

Elephant Rocks State Park

Kilometer
0   0.2
Mile
0   0.2

N

Engine House Ruins Trail

Quarry

Braille Trail

Service
Area

53

P

5

To
Belleview
5 miles

Quarry

21

To
Graniteville

0.4 The trail makes a sharp turn to the left (west) and passes a spur trail to the right (north) that leads to the Engine House ruins.

0.5 Turn left (south) onto the spur trail to the overlook area. Return to main trail.

0.8 Come to the quarry overlook.

1.0 Reach the end of the loop; turn right (south).

1.1 Arrive back at the trailhead.

6 Taum Sauk Mountain State Park: Mina Sauk Falls Loop Trail/ Ozark Trail to Devil's Tollgate

Taum Sauk Mountain State Park boasts both Missouri's highest point and its tallest waterfall. A visit to the highpoint first, then Mina Sauk Falls, followed by a hike down to the rock formation known as Devil's Tollgate makes this hike a nice little trifecta.

Distance: 5.1-mile lollipop
Hiking time: About 3 hours
Difficulty: More challenging due to steep climb and rugged terrain
Best season: Spring and fall
Other trail users: None
Canine compatibility: Leashed dogs permitted
Fees and permits: No fees or permits required
Maps: USGS Ironton; Ozark Trail—Taum Sauk Section map available at the trailhead

Trail contacts: Johnson's Shut-Ins State Park, 148 Taum Sauk Trail, Middlebrook 63656; (573) 546-2450; http://mostateparks .com/jshutins.htm
Special considerations: The trail is very rugged, and the return portion of the hike requires a steep climb. Snakes, ticks, and mosquitoes are common during summer.

Finding the trailhead: From Ironton drive 4.9 miles on MO 21 south. After 4.9 miles reach State Road CC and the signed turn for Taum Sauk Mountain State Park. Turn right (west) onto State Road CC and continue 3.6 miles to the parking area. GPS: N37 34.369' / W90 43.700'

The Hike

Located in the St. Francois Mountains, Taum Sauk Mountain State Park is one of the most rugged and beautiful locations in the state. Formed over one billion years ago, this area was created when volcanic eruptions of hot ash settled and cooled to form rhyolite.

Traces of these mountains still remain, although they are now covered in hardwood forests of oak and hickory trees. The highest point in Missouri, Taum Sauk Mountain's elevation is 1,772 feet. This rugged day hike leads you past the state's highest point and its tallest wet-weather waterfall. You will also be on part of the longest trail in the state, the 350-mile-long Ozark Trail. The turnaround point for this hike is Devil's Tollgate, a hunk of volcanic rhyolite that stands over 30 feet tall.

The trailhead for Mina Sauk Falls Loop Trail is located at the southwest corner of the Taum Sauk Mountain parking area. Begin hiking southwest on the trail and reach a fork at 0.2 mile. Left will take you to the Missouri Highpoint; continue right (southwest) to a second fork at 0.3 mile to a trailhead register. Left is the Mina Sauk Falls Loop return trail; stay right (southwest) as the trail becomes more rocky and rugged and descends slightly. Reach the junction of the Mina Sauk Falls and Ozark Trails at 1.4 miles and bear right (southwest) onto the Ozark Trail.

The trail makes a steep descent down to the base of Mina Sauk Falls at 1.6 miles and continues on to the Devil's Tollgate at 2.4 miles. After taking a few pictures return to the Mina Sauk Falls Loop Trail/Ozark Trail junction and turn right (east) to continue past the falls and continue the loop.

Reach a fork at 4.5 miles. The Mina Sauk Falls Loop Trail leads to the left (northwest) and continues to the trailhead register at 4.8 miles. Turn right (northeast) at the fork and reach another fork at 4.9 miles; stay left (northeast) to return to the trailhead.

Miles and Directions

0.0   Start at the trailhead and hike southeast on the Mina Sauk Falls Loop Trail.

0.2   Come to a fork in the trail and turn right (northeast). (**Option:** The left fork leads to the highest point in Missouri.)

0.3 Reach a second fork and the trailhead register; stay right (northeast), heading toward Mina Sauk Falls.

1.4 The Mina Sauk Falls Trail connects with the Ozark Trail. A left (east) turn here leads to Mina Sauk Falls and continues the loop. For now turn right (west) onto the Ozark Trail toward the Devil's Tollgate, following the OT's white-and-green blazes.

1.6 Pass the base of Mina Sauk Falls.

2.4 Reach the Devil's Tollgate; return to Mina Sauk Falls.

3.8 Return to the junction of Mina Sauk Falls Loop and Ozark Trails. Turn right (east) to continue on the Mina Sauk Falls/Ozark Trail.

4.5 Reach junction of Ozark and Mina Sauk Falls Loop Trails. Turn left (northwest) to complete the Mina Sauk Falls Loop Trail.

4.8 Reach the trailhead register; turn right (northeast).

4.9 Return to the first fork and stay left (northeast).

5.1 Arrive back at the trailhead.

7 Amidon Memorial Conservation A[rea]: Cedar Glade Trail

Amidon Memorial Conservation Area offers one of the only granite shut-ins in Missouri. The pink granite rocks make the area a popular swimming hole during summer, and the Cedar Glade Trail explores some of the area's more interesting features.

Distance: 1.0-mile loop
Hiking time: 30 minutes (plan on spending more time if you wish to explore the shut-ins)
Difficulty: Easy
Best season: Year-round
Other trail users: None
Canine compatibility: Leashed dogs permitted
Fees and permits: No fees or permits required
Maps: USGS Fredericktown

Trail contacts: Missouri Department of Conservation, Southeast Regional Office, 2302 County Park Dr., Cape Girardeau 63701; (573) 290-5730; www.mdc.mo .gov
Special considerations: Conservation areas are closed from 10 p.m. to 4 a.m. except for authorized camping, fishing, and hunting activities.

Finding the trailhead: From Fredericktown drive 1.9 miles east on MO 72. After 1.9 miles turn left (northeast) onto State Road J. Continue on J for 4.4 miles to State Road W. Turn right (south) onto State Road W and drive 1.2 miles. Turn left (east) onto CR 208 and continue 1.1 miles. Turn left (north) onto CR 253 and drive 0.8 mile to the parking area on the right. GPS: N37 34.141' / W90 9.3'

Located in Bollinger and Madison Counties, the 1,632-acre Amidon Memorial Conservation Area is a fantastic destination almost any time of year. Locally the area is often referred to as either Pink Rocks or Hahns Mill. The first nickname obviously refers to the main geological feature in the area, while Hahns Mill refers to the historic grain mill that stood here in the late 1800s.

The crystal-clear waters of the Castor River flow through the incredibly pink granite shut-ins, forming natural slides, waterfalls, and swimming holes. Visit at sunset to watch the picturesque granite glow in shades of pink, orange, and purple. The rocks radiate warmth after baking in the sun all day, making it an enjoyable destination even on cool days.

The mostly hardwood forest is dominated by oak, hickory, and maple, although you will also see white ash, black gum, and sassafras. Growing along the steep banks of the Castor River, shortleaf pine and eastern red cedar punctuate the skyline. Look for prickly pear cactus and the purple blooms of wild hyacinth as you cross through glade restoration areas.

The 1.0-mile Cedar Glade Trail is a great place to begin your exploration of this area. The natural-surface trail begins on the eastern side of the parking area and traverses a field, which provides a food source for area wildlife area.

At 0.1 mile the trail forks; stay left (east) as the trail winds through the hardwood forest until it reaches the banks of the Castor River and shut-ins at 0.3 mile. Here you will want to leave the trail to explore the rocks, wade, swim, picnic, or just enjoy the natural beauty of the area. After taking in the

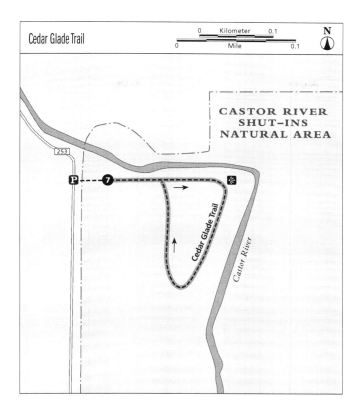

CASTOR RIVER
SHUT–INS
NATURAL AREA

Cedar Glade Trail

Castor River

sights, return to the trail as it parallels the river for a short time before turning right (southwest) into the forest.

At 0.7 mile cross two footbridges.

At 0.85 mile come to the end of the loop and turn left (west) to return to the trailhead and parking area.

Miles and Directions

0.0   Start at the trailhead and hike east on the natural-surface trail.

0.1	Come to a fork in the trail; continue left (east).
0.3	Reach the shut-ins area.
0.7	Cross two footbridges.
0.85	Come to the end of the loop; turn left (west).
1.0	Arrive back at the trailhead and parking area.

8 Cape Girardeau Conservation Nature Center Trails

Located within the city limits of Cape Girardeau the Cape Girardeau Conservation Nature Center is a spectacular resource for people hoping to learn more about the nature of southeastern Missouri and the Ozarks. In addition to the stellar educational and interpretive information and programs offered here, the nature center also offers several options for hiking. Linked together, these trails form a fantastic loop hike.

Distance: 1.4-mile loop
Hiking time: About 1.5 hours
Difficulty: Easy due to length
Best season: Year-round
Other trail users: None
Canine compatibility: No pets allowed
Fees and permits: No fees or permits required
Schedule: Trails open daily from sunrise to 10 p.m.; nature center open Tues–Sat from 8 a.m. to 5 p.m.; closed Sun and Mon, Thanksgiving Day and the following Fri, Christmas Day, and New Year's Day
Maps: USGS Cape Girardeau; detailed trail map and brochure available at the nature center.
Trail contacts: Cape Girardeau Conservation Nature Center, 2289 County Park Dr., Cape Girardeau 63701; (573) 290-5218; http://mdc.mo .gov/regions/southeast/cape-girardeau-conservation-nature-center

Finding the trailhead: From Cape Girardeau drive 3.2 miles on North Kingshighway Street to the entrance for the Cape Girardeau Conservation Nature Center. Turn right (northeast) onto County Park

Drive and continue 0.3 mile to the nature center parking area. GPS: N37 20.626' / W89 35.418'

The Hike

Managed by the Missouri Department of Conservation, the Cape Girardeau Conservation Nature Center is a great place to spend the day. Inside the nature center, visitors will find programs, activities, and displays that focus on the nature of southeastern Missouri and the Ozarks. Offering a wide range of activities that are geared for children, teens, adults, and families, the nature center is an incredible resource for nature enthusiasts living in or visiting the area.

Outside the nature center, explore the nature trails that take you over rolling hills, through dense hardwood woodlands, into deep hollows, and past interesting topographical features known as sinkholes. The flora, fauna, and landscape here are much like what you would expect to see on the eastern border of the Ozarks. Hikers will likely see lots of wildlife along the trails; white-tailed deer, wild turkey, eastern gray squirrel, bullfrogs, and box turtles are common sights here. Fox, muskrat, bobcat, raccoon and other Ozark critters also can be found here, although they may be a bit more challenging to spot. Visit anytime except winter and you are sure to see an array of wildflowers, including purple coneflower and Queen Anne's lace.

While there are several short, easy trails in the conservation area, the 2.25-mile outer loop allows visitors to gain a broader appreciation of the natural diversity of the area. To begin this hike, find the Ridgetop Trailhead, located on the west side of the nature center.

Begin hiking south on the paved Ridgetop Trail, passing behind the nature center and continuing southeast. At 0.3

mile turn right (south) onto the Paw Paw Valley Trail. As its name suggests, this moderate gravel trail take you past many pawpaw trees. The pawpaw is a relatively small tree with bright green leaves that produces fruit similar in size and shape to a small banana. While edible for humans, the chief consumer of pawpaws is wildlife, and you may see opossums, squirrels, or raccoons feasting on the soft, custard-flavored pulp.

The Paw Paw Valley Trail takes you over several bridges and an intermittent stream before coming to a trail intersection at 0.55 mile.

Bear right (northeast) onto the Sinkhole Bottom Trail. You will notice a paved trail splitting off to the right (east) just after the trail intersection. This walking/running/biking trail is the Cape LaCroix Recreation Trail. Continue on the gravel Sinkhole Bottom Trail, looking for the sinkhole on the right (east) side of the trail. Sinkholes are usually caused by the collapse of an underground cavern and are a common feature of the karst topography here in the Ozarks. The Sinkhole Bottom Tail is the steepest portion of this loop hike, and your heart rate will likely be elevated by the time you reach the next trail intersection at 0.85 mile.

Turn right (northwest) onto the Tulip Poplar Hill Trail. Hikers will easily spot tulip poplars during summer. Also known as yellow poplars, these beautiful, tall trees have large tuliplike flowers that are orange and green.

At 1.05 miles come to another trail intersection; turn right (north) to visit Wood Duck Swamp. Technically an old lagoon, the swamp is a good place to spot herons and muskrats, so it's worth seeing. After visiting the swamp, return to the junction and turn right to continue on Tulip Poplar Hill Trail. Reach Cottonwood Crossing at 1.2 miles. Turn left

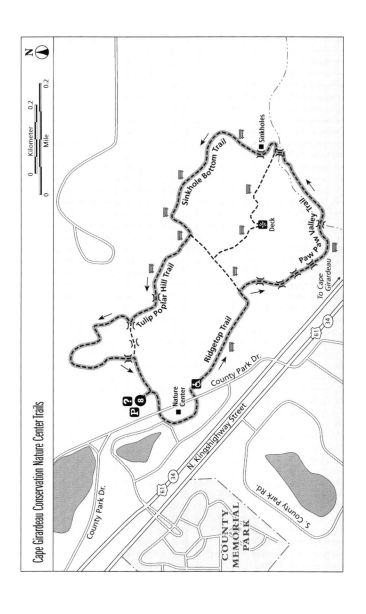

(south) to return to the Tulip Poplar Hill Trail. The trail to the right (north) leads to the paved Maple Hollow Trail.

At 1.3 miles return to the Tulip Poplar Trail; turn right (southwest), following the gravel trail back to the nature center. At 1.4 miles arrive back at the Cape Girardeau Conservation Nature Center.

Miles and Directions

0.0 Start at the Ridgetop Trailhead, located on the west side of the nature center, and begin hiking south.

0.3 Turn right (south) onto the Paw Paw Valley Trail.

0.55 Bear right (northeast) onto the Sinkhole Bottom Trail.

0.85 Turn right (northwest) onto the Tulip Poplar Hill Trail.

1.05 Turn right (north) to visit Wood Duck Swamp. Return to the junction and turn right to continue on Tulip Poplar Hill Trail.

1.2 Turn left (south) at Cottonwood Crossing to return to the Tulip Poplar Hill Trail.

1.3 Reach the Tulip Poplar Hill Trail.

1.4 Arrive back at the Cape Girardeau Conservation Nature Center.

9 Sam A. Baker State Park: Shut-Ins Trail

This out-and-back trail traverses a bottomland forest before climbing a tall bluff overlooking Big Creek and the surrounding Ozark hillsides. Fantastic views and a short side trip to a great swimming hole make this an excellent day trip.

Distance: 2.4 miles out and back

Hiking time: About 1.5 hours (Allow additional time if you plan to go swimming.)

Difficulty: Moderate due to modest climb

Best season: Year-round

Other trail users: None

Canine compatibility: Leashed dogs permitted

Fees and permits: No fees or permits required

Maps: USGS Brunot; park map available at the park office, visitor center, and on the park's website

Trail contacts: Sam A. Baker State Park, Route 1, Box 113, Patterson 63956; (573) 856-4411 or (573) 856-4223; http://mostateparks.com/park/sam-baker-state-park

Special considerations: Ticks and chiggers are common in warmer months.

Finding the trailhead: From Piedmont drive 9.7 miles east on MO 34. Turn left (north) onto MO 143 and continue 5.8 miles to the trailhead parking area on the right (east). GPS: N37 15.611' / W90 30.385'

The Hike

One of Missouri's oldest state parks, Sam A. Baker State Park has become an iconic family destination for many Missouri families. Sam A. Baker State Park typifies the classic Missouri state park experience, and each year new visitors adopt the tradition of enjoying family, friends, and nature in these beautiful Ozark hills.

The park is named for former Missouri governor Samuel Aaron Baker, who advocated for its creation in the 1920s. Witnessing the natural beauty here, it is easy to see why he hoped to preserve the area for generations to come. Like much of the Ozarks, domelike knobs, valleys, exposed cliff bluffs, hardwood forests, and glades characterize the park's rugged landscape.

Similar to several other early Missouri state parks, this park offers visitors a unique outdoor experience. Rustic cabins, a dining lodge, picnic shelters, and several hiking shelter showcase the craftsmanship of the Civilian Conservation Corp, which worked here during the 1930s. In addition to hiking, visitors enjoy biking, horseback riding, camping, swimming, and backpacking. The park provides access to both the St. Francois River and Big Creek, making canoeing, kayaking, and fishing popular pastimes here. Crappie, smallmouth bass, and catfish are just a few of the fish species that make their home in these cool, clear waters.

The trail begins on the northwest end of the stone dining lodge, which offers breakfast, lunch, and dinner from Memorial Day through Labor Day (check the park's website for hours). Behind the lodge, the trail descends steep stairs and traverses the bottomland forest along Big Creek. At 0.1 mile you come to a wooden footbridge across a small drainage and continue northeast. Look for white-tailed deer, turkeys, and squirrels, which are common throughout the park. Visitors may also see bobcats, raccoons, and opossums, which are more commonly sighted in the evening.

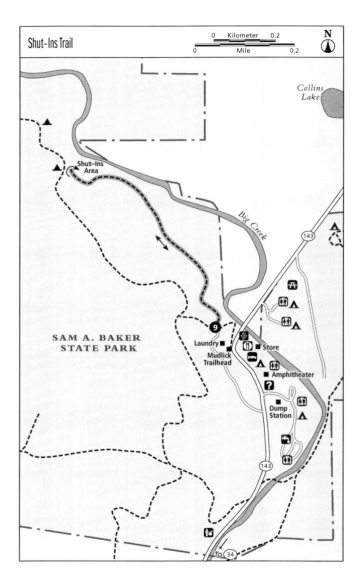

Shut–Ins Trail

Kilometer

Mile

N

Collins Lake

Shut–Ins Area

Big Creek

9

SAM A. BAKER
STATE PARK

Laundry

Mudlick
Trailhead

Store

Amphitheater

Dump
Station

To 34

143

143

At 0.8 mile come to a fork in the trail; stay right and continue hiking northwest. Oak, hickory, sycamore, and cottonwood trees can be found along the trail. Also keep an eye out for the yellowwood tree, easily identified in spring by its striking white, occasionally pink, blooms.

After hiking 1.0 mile stay alert and look for an angled blue trail marker and a fork in the trail. The trail to the left (west) climbs a steep ridge 0.2 mile to the camping shelter at the top of the ridge. The right-hand trail heads east to the banks of Big Creek, which is well worth a detour to enjoy its crystal-clear waters. To continue the hike, bear left at the fork and climb the ridge (if you reach the Big Creek, you've gone too far and need to backtrack to the fork).

Once you've reached the camping shelter, take a moment to enjoy the view of the surrounding Ozark hillside. At this point, 1.2 miles, the Shut-Ins Trail joins the 17-mile Mudlick Trail. The Mudlick Trail, a designated National Recreation Trail, traverses the 4,420-acre Mudlick Mountain Wild Area and the 1,370-acre Mudlick Natural Area and is an excellent choice for a longer, more strenuous backpacking trip. After enjoying the stunning ridgetop views, return to the lodge and trailhead via the same route.

Miles and Directions

0.0   Start at the dining lodge and begin hiking northwest.

0.1   Cross a footbridge and continue northwest.

0.8   Come to a fork in the trail; stay right and continue northwest.

1.0   Bear left (west) at the fork and climb a steep ridge. (**Option:** Take the right-hand fork to enjoy a swim in Big Creek.)

1.2   Reach the stone camping shelter and intersection with the Mudlick Trail. Return to the trailhead via the same route.

2.4   Arrive back at the trailhead and dining lodge.

10 Ozark National Scenic Riverways: Spring Branch Trail

Located just south of Van Buren, Big Spring offers hikers and sightseers an amazing opportunity. The spring is the largest in Missouri, considered by many to be the largest in the United States, and one of the largest springs in the world. The Spring Branch Trail offers prime viewing.

Distance: 0.8 mile out and back

Hiking time: About 30 minutes

Difficulty: Easy due to short, flat trail

Best season: Fall

Other trail users: None

Canine compatibility: Leashed dogs permitted

Fees and permits: No fees or permits required

Maps: USGS Big Spring; trail map available at the trailhead

Trail contacts: Ozark National Scenic Riverways, 404 Watercress Dr., Van Buren 63965; (573) 323-4236; www.nps.gov/ozar/planyourvisit/big-spring.htm

Special considerations: Ticks and mosquitoes are common during warmer months.

Finding the trailhead: From Van Buren drive south on MO 103 for 3.8 miles to where the road becomes Pea Vine Road. Continue straight and drive 0.4 mile on Pea Vine Road to the Big Spring Trails parking area on the left (north). GPS: N36 57.184' / W90 59.586'

The Hike

Big Spring was actually one of Missouri's first state parks before it became a national park. The area was a state park from 1924 to 1969, when it was donated by the people of

Missouri to the National Park Service to become part of the Ozark National Scenic Riverways. Big Spring pumps out an astonishing 286 million gallons of water a day. A day! Depending on rainfall in the area, it can pump out even more, making it one of the largest springs in the United States. It competes with the Snake River Spring in Idaho and Florida's Silver Spring for top honors. Experts say that the three springs are probably very close to the same size and take turns being the largest depending on current rainfall.

Not only does the spring unleash a whopping 286 million gallons of water each day, but it also pumps out an estimated 70 tons of dissolved limestone each day. The karst region surrounding the spring could become an unbelievably large cave if the spring were ever to dry up. Underground passageways direct water to Big Spring from as far away as 50 miles.

The Big Spring State Natural Area offers visitors numerous options for recreation. A campground has both tent and RV sites, and several picnic areas are scattered around the park. People preferring lodging can opt for the Big Spring Lodge and cabins that were built by the Civilian Conservation Corps. Activities include horseback riding, birding, canoeing, and of course hiking. Hikes in the area include the Slough, Stone Ridge, Chubb Hollow, and Spring Branch Trails. Many of these trails can be connected to make a longer day hike. The Spring Branch Trail is highlighted here.

When you pull up to the parking lot, Big Spring is clearly visible from your vehicle. The enormous amount of water that flows from the spring literally spews from the ground and can be quite breathtaking when you first see it. The Spring Branch Trail starts at the Big Spring Trails kiosk, located at the parking area.

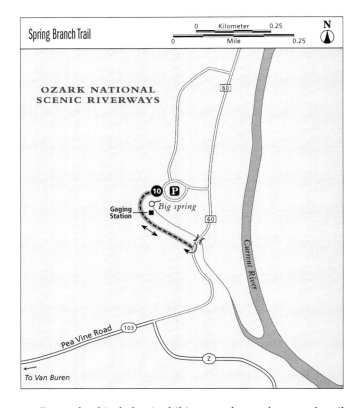

OZARK NATIONAL
SCENIC RIVERWAYS

Gaging
Station

Big spring

Current River

Pea Vine Road

To Van Buren

From the kiosk begin hiking south on the paved trail directly toward Big Spring. After just 0.1 mile you will reach the spring and the overlook area. As you approach the spring, it will feel like someone turned on the air conditioner if you are visiting during the hot summer months. The cool air alone that flows off the water makes the trip worthwhile.

After taking in the scenery, continue on the trail as it circles the spring and meanders into the woods. At 0.2 mile you pass a spur trail that branches to the left (north) and simply takes hikers down for another view of the spring. Continue straight past the spur trail and reach a fork at 0.4 mile. The left fork leads to the road and a picnic area; the right fork leads to the Chubb Hollow Trail. Turn around here and return to the trailhead via the same route for another view of the Big Spring.

Miles and Directions

0.0 Start at the Big Spring Trails kiosk and begin hiking south on the paved trail.

0.1 Reach the Big Spring overlook and cave area; continue hiking southeast.

0.2 A spur trail breaks off to the left (north); stay right (southeast).

0.4 Come to a fork in the trail; retrace your steps to the trailhead.

0.8 Arrive back at the trailhead.

11 Blue Spring Natural Area: Blue Spring Trail

According to local legend, the people of the Osage tribe called this spring the "Spring of the Summer Sky." This trail follows the banks of the Current River to the deepest spring in the state of Missouri.

Distance: 3.0 miles out and back

Hiking time: About 1.5 hours

Difficulty: Easy

Best season: Year-round

Other trail users: None

Canine compatibility: Leashed dogs permitted

Fees and permits: No fees or permits required

Maps: USGS Eminence; park map available park office

Trail contacts: Missouri Department of Conservation—Southeast Regional Office, 2302 County Park Dr., Cape Girardeau 63701; (573) 290-5730; www.mdc.mo.gov

Ozark National Scenic Riverways, 404 Watercress Dr., Van Buren 63965; (573) 323-4236; www.nps.gov/ozar/planyourvisit/big-spring.htm

Special considerations: Ticks and chiggers are common in warmer months.

Finding the trailhead: From the small town of Eminence drive east on MO 106 for 13.4 miles. Turn right (south) onto CR 531 toward the Powder Mill Campground and continue 0.6 mile to the parking area on the left (east). GPS: N37 10.935' / W91 10.477'

The Hike

This easy day hike will take you to one of the most beautiful springs in the United States. The turquoise-hued waters of the aptly named Blue Spring make a wonderful hike for those lucky enough to visit this part of the Ozarks. While slightly longer than the traditional path to Blue Spring, this out-and-back trail follows the banks of the Current River and gives hikers the opportunity to enjoy the area's diverse flora and fauna.

Blue Spring has as average daily flow of around ninety million gallons, making it only the sixth-largest spring in Missouri. This impressive flow is responsible for the formation of underground caves and water passages as the rushing water dissolves limestone and dolomite. At 300 feet it does hold the record for being the deepest spring in the state, and it is certainly one of the most visually stunning springs you are ever likely to see.

The spring's color is a result in part of its extreme depth, as well as minerals, such as limestone and dolomite, and organic matter that are suspended in the water.

Blue Spring offers a nice hike any time of the year, although spring and fall are particularly pleasant. Spring hikers will be treated to displays of Ozark wildflowers that grow along the river, spring, and steep bluffs that surround the spring. Those visiting in fall will be impressed by the contrast of the water with the firey display of orange, red, and yellow leaves of the turning trees. Other factors such as cloud cover and rainfall can temporarily affect the water's color, but it is always stunning.

While completely surrounded by National Park Service land, the 17-acre Blue Spring Natural Area is owned by the Missouri Department of Conservation. Both agencies provide interpretive information about the area.

From the trailhead at the Powder Mill Campground, begin hiking southeast on the obvious dirt path through

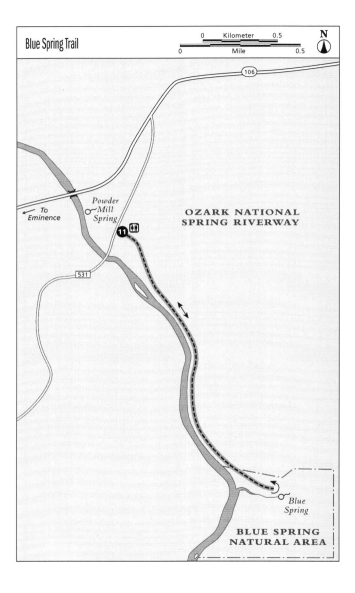

Blue Spring Trail

OZARK NATIONAL
SPRING RIVERWAY

106

To
Eminence

Powder
Mill
Spring

11

531

Blue
Spring

BLUE SPRING
NATURAL AREA

N

Kilometer
0   0.5
Mile
0   0.5

bottomland woodland. After a short distance the trail begins to parallel the Current River and basically follows the river until the trail reaches Blue Spring overlook. Look for trees such as sycamore, box elder, and river birch, all of which can withstand periodic flooding.

At 0.36 mile cross a wooden footbridge over a small drainage and continue hiking southeast along the banks of the Current River, which is part of the Ozark National Scenic Riverways and managed by the National Park Service. Come to a rest bench at 0.65 mile.

At 1.2 miles come to a fork in the trail; stay right (southeast) to continue along the Current River toward Blue Spring. At 1.5 miles reach Blue Spring overlook. Return to the trailhead and parking area at Powder Mill Campground via the same route.

Miles and Directions

0.0   Start at the Powder Mill Campground parking area and begin hiking southeast on the obvious dirt trail.

0.36   Cross a footbridge; continue southeast.

1.2   Stay right (southeast) at the fork.

1.5   Reach Blue Spring overlook. Return the way you came.

3.0   Arrive back at Powder Mill Campground.

12 Ozark Trail: Klepzig Mill to Rocky Falls

This 3.1-mile section of the Ozark Trail begins at beautiful Klepzig Mill and shut-ins and ends at the equally impressive Rocky Falls.

Distance: 3.1-mile shuttle
Hiking time: About 2 hours
Difficulty: Moderate due to terrain
Best season: Fall through spring
Other trail users: None
Canine compatibility: Leashed dogs permitted
Fees and permits: No fees or permits required

Maps: USGS Stegall Mountain
Trail contacts: Ozark National Scenic Riverways, 404 Watercress Dr., P.O. Box 490, Van Buren 63965; (573) 323-4236
Special considerations: Ticks and poison ivy are common in warmer months.

Finding the trailhead: To Klepzig Mill: From Eminence drive east on MO 106 for 7 miles. Turn right (south) onto State Road H and continue driving for 4 miles. Turn left (east) onto State Road NN and drive 4.2 miles until you reach Shannon CR 522, which forks to the left (north). Drive 1.3 miles to the trailhead parking on the left (south).

To Rocky Falls: From Eminence drive east on MO 106 for 7 miles. Turn right (south) onto State Road H and continue driving for 4 miles. Turn left (east) onto State Road NN and drive 0.5 mile. Turn right (south) on to CR 526. Continue 0.1 mile and turn left (east) into the parking area signed for Rocky Falls. GPS: N37 7.581' / W91 11.937'

The Hike

This section of the Ozark Trail makes an excellent day hike for those looking to explore the exceptional beauty of the Ozarks. The trail begins near Klepzig Mill and shut-ins. On the National Register of Historic Places, the small turbine mill was constructed in 1928 by Walter Klepzig. There is also a series of small shut-ins in this area. Although smaller in size than other shut-ins found in the region, such as Johnson's Shut-ins, the area is well worth a visit any time of year.

At the southern end of this trail, where you will leave your shuttle vehicle, lies Rocky Falls, an impressive 40-foot waterfall that cascades over a series of rhyolite steps. During hot weather you will likely find the area crowded with swimmers. While it is an excellent swimming hole, if you are looking for solitude, visit during cooler weather.

From the trailhead begin hiking south on the rocky doubletrack path, following the green-and-white Ozark Trail markers. The trail shortly returns to the banks of Rocky Creek, which provides amazing scenery and offers ample opportunities for wading in the cool, clear creek.

At 0.86 mile come to some shut-ins and enjoy the scenery as you pass between Mill and Buzzard Mountains. Pay close attention as the trail climbs a small hill at 0.94 mile; it is easy to miss. This small doubletrack trail reaches State Road NN at 1.18 miles. Turn right (southwest) and walk along the side of the road for a short distance. Cross Rocky Creek again at 1.6 miles and look for the green-and-white OZARK TRAIL markers on the left (south) side of the road.

Leave State Road NN and hike south on the Ozark Trail, passing through a small grove of eastern red cedars and coming to a grassy clearing at 1.7 miles. Here the scenery

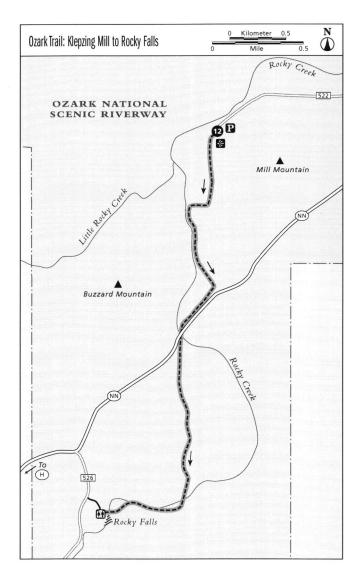

Ozark Trail: Klepzing Mill to Rocky Falls

OZARK NATIONAL
SCENIC RIVERWAY

Rocky Creek

522

12 P

Mill Mountain

NN

Little Rocky Creek

Buzzard Mountain

Rocky Creek

NN

To
H

526

Rocky Falls

is quite different from the mostly hardwood forest you just left. Count on seeing a variety of wildflowers here much of the year.

At 2.57 miles cross the creek and continue on the trail to a trail intersection at 2.64 miles. Turn right (west) here and follow the grassy path to Rocky Falls. Reach the Rocky Falls parking area at 3.1 miles. A paved walkway leads to the falls. Pick up your shuttle vehicle at the falls parking lot.

Miles and Directions

0.0 Start at the small parking area at Klepzig Mill and begin hiking south on the rocky doubletrack.

0.86 Reach shut-ins.

0.94 The trail climbs a small hill.

1.18 Come to State Road NN; turn right (southwest) and follow the road.

1.6 Cross Rocky Creek; turn left (south) onto the Ozark Trail.

2.57 Cross a creek.

2.64 Come to a spur trail to Rocky Falls; turn right (west) onto a spur trail.

3.1 Arrive at the Rocky Falls parking area and pick up your shuttle.

13 Ozark National Scenic Riverways: Alley Spring Nature Trails

Located just minutes from the small base camp town of Eminence Alley Spring offers nature lovers an ideal spot to spend an hour or an entire day. Alley Spring offers a picnic area, historic buildings, horseback riding trails, and hiking trails.

Distance: 1.8-mile lollipop
Hiking time: About 1 to 1.5 hours
Difficulty: Moderate due to a steep climb
Best season: Year-round
Other trail users: None
Canine compatibility: Leashed dogs permitted
Fees and permits: No fees or permits required

Maps: USGS Alley Spring; trail map available at visitor center
Trail contacts: Ozark National Scenic Riverways, 404 Watercress Dr., Van Buren 63965; (573) 323-4236; www.nps.gov/ozar/planyourvisit/big-spring.htm
Special considerations: Ticks and mosquitoes are common during warmer months.

Finding the trailhead: From Eminence drive 5.7 miles west on MO 106 to the parking area for Alley Spring and Alley Spring Mill. Turn right (east) into the parking area. GPS: N37 9.094' / W91 26.526'

The Hike

Alley Spring measures about 32 feet deep and 60 feet wide and pours out around 81 million gallons of water daily. The fragile ecosystem around the spring is home to numerous species of wildlife including snails, minnows, mink, muskrat, and snakes. A series of connected hiking trails surrounds the spring and the area, and numerous picnic sites are scattered throughout the grounds.

For hundreds of years the people of the Missouri Ozarks have used Alley Spring as a place for both social and economic gatherings. The mill was built in 1894 by George Washington McCaskill as a merchant mill for the surrounding farmlands. The additions of a schoolhouse, church, and homes made Alley Spring a place where people could come together and socialize at dances, baseball games, and picnics.

Today the spring is still an ideal place for social gatherings. The Alley Spring Campground hosts over 160 sites that are ideal for family camping. Picnic areas around the spring and mill provide opportunities for groups to get together and enjoy meals, while the horseback and hiking trails offer nice, leisurely rides and strolls to families and nature lovers.

The Alley Spring Nature Trails are a short network of trails that offer a lot of amazing views for a short amount of time and energy. From the Alley Spring parking area, begin hiking north on the paved sidewalk. A large picnic pavilion, restrooms with flush toilets, and a playground are on the left (west). At 0.1 mile reach a wooden bridge. Turn right (east) to cross the bridge and head toward the mill. Those interested in some of the historical buildings in the area can turn left (west) to visit the old schoolhouse before crossing the bridge. After crossing the bridge turn left (north) to continue toward the mill. You reach the Alley Spring Mill after just 0.2 mile. Take time to check out the mill, which is now a visitor center.

After taking in the mill's rich history, stay left to hike on the Overlook Trail. Circle around to the north side of the mill and begin climbing a steep rocky hill to an overlook

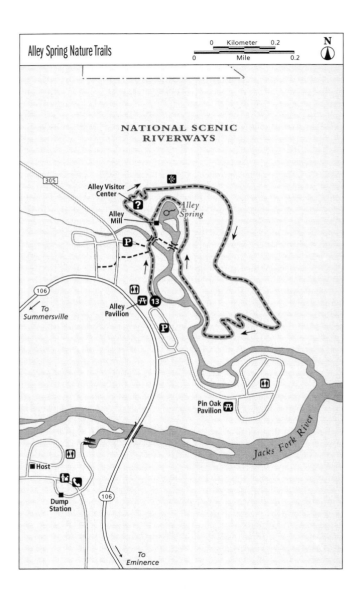

Alley Spring Nature Trails

0   Kilometer   0.2
0   Mile   0.2

N

NATIONAL SCENIC
RIVERWAYS

305

Alley Visitor
Center

Alley Mill

Alley
Spring

P

106

To
Summersville

Alley
Pavilion

13

P

Pin Oak
Pavilion

Jacks Fork River

Host

Dump
Station

106

To
Eminence

area. Reach the overlook at 0.5 mile. An interpretive sign and viewing area sits above the mill and looks down over the spring. Fall colors are worth the hike!

Finish taking in the scenery and begin hiking south along the ridgeline to continue the loop portion of the trail. After descending the ridge, you reach a set of stairs at 1.2 miles that lead to the North River Road and a horse-hitching rail. Continue west past the hitching rail and reach the Spring Branch Trail at 1.3 miles.

Turn right (north) onto the Spring Branch Trail and hike north toward Alley Spring. At 1.5 miles you come to a bridge that crosses the branch and offers a shorter hike. Stay right here; continue hiking around the spring to take in some up-close views. Reach the end of the loop portion of the hike and return to the mill at 1.6 miles. Turn left and retrace your route to the trailhead.

Miles and Directions

0.0   Start at the parking area and begin hiking north on the paved sidewalk.

0.1   Turn right (east) to cross a bridge toward Alley Mill; turn left (north) after crossing the bridge.

0.2   Reach Alley Mill; stay left (north) on the Overlook Trail to begin the loop.

0.5   Come to the Alley Spring overlook.

1.2   Reach a set of stairs that descend west to an old road and area for horse trailers.

1.3   Turn right (north) onto Spring Branch Trail to follow the creek.

1.5   Come to a bridge; stay right on the trail to circle the spring. (**Option:** Cross the bridge to shorten your hike.)

1.6   Reach the end of loop; turn left to return to trailhead.

1.8   Arrive back at the trailhead.

14 **Roaring River State Park: Devil's Kitchen Trail**

Named for a strange rock outcropping that once formed a roomlike enclosure, the Devil's Kitchen Trail is a fun day hike and a good opportunity to explore the interesting geography that is common to this part of Missouri.

Distance: 1.5-mile loop
Hiking time: About 1.5 hours
Difficulty: Moderate due to modest climbs
Best season: Year-round
Other trail users: None
Canine compatibility: Leashed dogs permitted
Fees and permits: No fees or permit required
Maps: USGS Eagle Rock; park map and self-guiding brochure

available at the park office and nature center
Trail contacts: Roaring River State Park, 12716 Farm Road 2239, Cassville 65625; (417) 847-2539; http://mostateparks.com/park/roaring-river-state-park
Special considerations: Ticks and chiggers are common in warmer months.

Finding the trailhead: From Cassville drive 6 miles on MO 112 to the park entrance. Continue on MO 112 for another 0.7 mile before turning left (north) onto CR 1135. Follow CR 1135 for 0.4 mile to parking area and trailhead. GPS: N36 35.448' / W93 50.092'

The Hike

Established in 1928, Roaring River State Park offers a wide variety of recreational activities. While best known for the trophy trout that swim the waters of Roaring River, the park also offers excellent opportunities for hiking, camping, swimming, and just enjoying the natural beauty of the area. Kids and adults alike will enjoy a visit to the fish hatchery and swimming pool.

The park is characterized by the type of terrain one would expect to find in the White River section of the Ozarks. Narrow valleys, deep blue springs, mountainlike topography, and interesting rock formations make the nearly 4,000-acre park the perfect day hiking destination. White-tailed deer, wild turkey, and gray fox are common here. The park is also home to several species that are rare or endangered in Missouri, including the Oklahoma salamander, the grotto salamander, the eastern collared lizard, and the black bear.

Devil's Kitchen Trail allows hikers a chance to view interesting geologic formations up close and personal. The trail begins in an oak-maple forest just west of the parking area. Hike northwest on the obvious rock trail. At 0.1 mile the trail splits, stay right (north) to follow the loop in a counterclockwise direction. Come to an area called The Bench at 0.16 mile. The Bench is an area where two different types of limestone rock meet. You can see that the lower rock, dolomite, is eroding much faster than the upper rock, forming a benchlike formation.

At 0.2 mile come to Shelter Cave—an example of the kind of cave used by bluff-dwellers nearly 10,000 years ago. Continue hiking north, reaching the top of the ridge at 0.6 mile.

As the trail begins to descend the ridge, notice the grove of shortleaf pine trees. This is the only native species of pine found in Missouri. Come to another cave, known as the Trailside Spring Cave, at 0.9 mile. This cave has a small

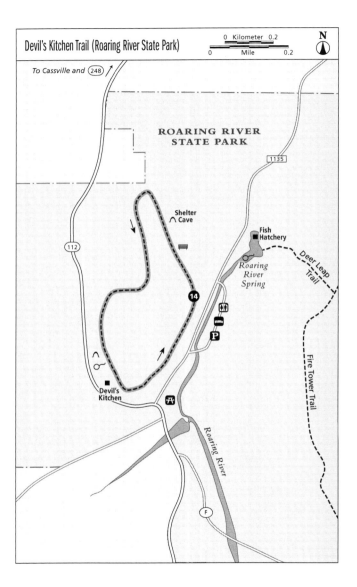

Devil's Kitchen Trail (Roaring River State Park)

0   Kilometer   0.2

0   Mile   0.2

N

To Cassville and 248

ROARING RIVER
STATE PARK

1135

112

Shelter
Cave

Fish
Hatchery

Roaring
River
Spring

Deer Leap Trail

14

P

Fire Tower Trail

Devil's
Kitchen

Roaring River

F

spring emerging from it and provides habitat for several types of creatures, including salamanders.

Just past the cave come to the headliner for this hike, Devil's Kitchen (0.93 mile). Take some time to explore the massive rocks before continuing east on the trail.

As you leave the Devil's Kitchen area, you may notice several "shortcuts" that bisect the longer switchbacks. Short-cutting switchbacks encourages erosion and trail washouts and kills habitat for plants and animals. Please stick to the main trail.

At 1.15 miles the trail forks; stay left (northeast) to return to the trailhead. Complete the loop portion of the hike at 1.35 miles; turn right and follow the trail back to the trail-head and parking area at 1.5 miles.

Miles and Directions

0.0	Start hiking northwest on the obvious rock trail.
0.1	The trail splits; stay right (north).
0.16	Come to the area known as The Bench.
0.2	Reach Shelter Cave.
0.6	Come to the top of the ridge.
0.9	Come to Trailside Spring Cave.
0.93	Reach the area known as Devil's Kitchen.
1.15	Come to a spur trail; stay left (northeast).
1.35	Complete the loop portion of the hike; turn right to return to the trailhead.
1.5	Arrive back at the trailhead.

15 Big Sugar Creek State Park: Ozark Chinquapin Trail

The Ozark Chinquapin Trail offers hikers a chance to experience the Elk River Breaks Natural Area. This remote trail offers solitude and the chance to see one of the best remaining upland savannas in Missouri.

Distance: 3.5-mile loop
Hiking time: About 2 hours
Difficulty: Moderate due to terrain
Best season: Fall through spring
Other trail users: None
Canine compatibility: Leashed dogs permitted
Fees and permits: No fees or permits required
Maps: USGS Noel

Trail contacts: Big Sugar Creek State Park, Big Sugar Creek Road, Pineville; (mailing address: c/o Roaring River State Park, Route 4, Box 4100, Cassville 65625); (417) 847-2539; http://mostateparks.com/park/big-sugar-creek-state-park
Special considerations: No drinking water is available. Ticks and poison ivy are common in warmer months.

Finding the trailhead: From the town of Pineville drive east on Eighth Street and continue 6.2 miles (Eighth Street becomes Big Sugar Creek Road) to the trailhead parking on the left (north). GPS: N36 37.29' / W94 17.653'

The Hike

Established in 1992, the 2,000-acre Big Sugar Creek State Park is the only Missouri state park that represents the Elk River Section of the Ozarks Natural Landscape Division.

Grassy upland prairies, thickly forested ridges, and savannas once dominated southwest Missouri. Now many of those areas have vanished—in particular, the areas known as savannas. Savannas are prairielike grasslands with few trees that require periodic fires to maintain their unique characteristics.

Big Sugar Creek State Park is probably the best remaining example of an upland savanna in the entire state. To further preserve the park's natural features, 1,613 acres of the park were designated as Elk River Breaks Natural Area by the Missouri Natural Areas Committee in 2000. Because this is a relatively new park, facilities are limited. When this guide went to press, there was a small information kiosk and outhouse at the trailhead. Plans are under way to further develop the park by adding a day-use area, interpretive structure, camping area, additional hiking trails, and a canoe launch.

The Ozark Chinquapin Trail winds through Elk River Breaks Natural Area. Hikers here can experience the landscape that makes this woodland so special. Shortleaf pine, oaks, and hickory trees grow along the grassy hillsides. Wildflowers including royal catchfly and purple coneflower can be found growing throughout the area. Solitude will be easy to find most of the year. In fact, the trail may feel a bit overgrown to the few hikers brave enough to visit in the hottest summer months.

From the parking area the trail heads north along a mowed grass pathway and soon enters the woodland. Look for the trail's namesake tree, the rare Ozark chinquapin, which is found only in the Ozarks. At 0.2 miles the trail forks; stay right (northeast) to follow the trail in a counterclockwise direction. Cross a shallow bedrock stream at 0.3 mile and continue hiking northeast as the trail begins

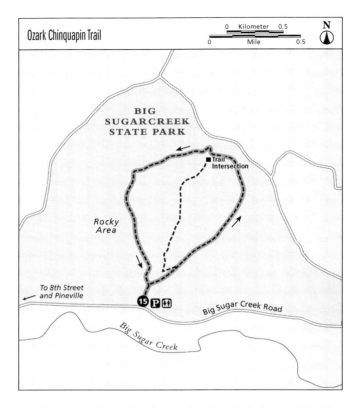

to climb into the upland woodland and glade. At 1.7 miles come the white-blazed Connector Trail, which leads back to the parking area. You can use this connector to shorten your hike. Continue northwest on the Ozark Chinquapin Trail to complete the full loop.

At 2.7 miles cross the rocky bedrock stream again and continue hiking southeast. Come to the end of the loop portion of the hike at 3.3 miles; turn right (south) and continue 0.2 mile to the trailhead and parking area.

Miles and Directions

0.0   Start at the gravel parking area and begin hiking north on the grass pathway.

0.2   The trail forks; stay right (northeast.

0.3   Cross a shallow bedrock stream.

1.7   Come to the Connector Trail; stay right (northwest) to continue on the Ozark Chinquapin Trail.

2.7   Cross the stream; continue hiking southeast.

3.3   Come to the end of the loop portion of the hike; turn right (south).

3.5   Arrive back at the trailhead and parking area.

16 **Pomme de Terre State Park: Indian Point Trail**

The Indian Point Trail offers a gentle stroll through a beautiful mixed-hardwood forest. The trail is highlighted by views of Pomme de Terre Lake from rocky and rugged Indian Point. Hikers wishing to make a day of the hike can stop by the picnic area and beach that can be accessed from the trail.

Distance: 3.1-mile loop
Hiking time: About 2 hours
Difficulty: Moderate due to length
Best season: Fall through spring
Other trail users: None
Canine compatibility: Leashed dogs permitted
Fees and permits: No fees or permits required

Schedule: Park open sunrise to sunset year-round
Maps: USGS Sentinel; trail maps available in the park office
Trail contacts: Pomme de Terre State Park, HC 77, Pittsburg 65724; (417) 852-4291; www .mostateparks.com/park/ pomme-de-terre-state-park
Special considerations: Ticks are common in warmer months.

Finding the trailhead: From Pittsburg drive 1.7 miles on MO 64 west to the MO 64 Spur. Turn left (northwest) onto MO 64 Spur and drive 1.9 miles into the park and to the parking area and trailhead on the left (west). GPS: N37 52.535' / W93 19.157'

The Hike

Pomme de Terre, literally translated as "apple of the earth," offers myriad recreational opportunities. The 734-acre state park contains an amazingly array of terrain, some of the best that the Missouri Ozarks have to offer. The rugged hills of the Springfield Plateau mixed with glades, the Pomme de Terre River, and the Pomme de Terre Lake afford recreational possibilities for land-lovers and water-lovers alike. The 200-year-old post oaks and chinquapin oaks that grow in abundance here are classic indicators not only of the rocky terrain but also that this area was once open woodland at the edge of the Great Plains.

Settlement of the area began in the 1830s, and the Pomme de Terre River was actually the divider between white settlers and the natives. The US Army Corps of Engineers dammed the spring-fed Pomme de Terre River in the early 1960s to create today's 7,800-acre Pomme de Terre Lake.

Visitors to Pomme de Terre State Park have a couple of options for a pleasant hike. On the Hermitage side of the park, hikers can enjoy a more heavily wooded area that follows rocky bluffs along the lake's shoreline. On the Pittsburg side of the park, where Indian Point Trail is located, hikers get to experience a trek through a savanna woodland. Both sides offer the opportunity to see wild turkeys, deer, purple finches, and prairie warblers.

The Indian Point Trail trailhead kiosk is located at the northern end of the trailhead parking area. Begin hiking north on the paved trail as it heads toward an outdoor amphitheater area; the pavement quickly ends and turns to a dirt surface. Continue hiking through the open woodland that is abundant with post and chinquapin oaks. At 0.4 mile cross the park road and continue hiking north into the woodland area. After 0.6 mile come to a picnic area on the left (west); turn sharply right (east) to continue on the Indian Point Trail. The trail continues for another

0.2 mile before reaching a restroom on the left (north), a park road (left goes to a beach area), and then a connector trail. After crossing the park road, headed east, pass the red connector trail that offers a shorter hike of about 1.5 miles. Continue hiking straight (northeast) to stay on the Indian Point Trail.

At 1.4 miles reach the spur trail that leads out to Indian Point. Take a few moments to walk out onto the rugged and rocky peninsula and take in the views before returning to the trail; continue south. After hiking through the woodland area and taking in several views of the lake, reach a bench at 2.7 miles that offers a nice place to rest while watching the folks down on the marina prep their boats.

Return to the trail and hike southwest for 0.3 mile before reaching the southern end of the red connector trail (3.0 miles). Continue hiking west past the connector trail and then across the park road. Return to the trailhead at 3.1 miles.

Miles and Directions

0.0   Start at the trailhead kiosk and travel left (north) on the Indian Point Trail, signed with blue arrows.

0.4   Cross the park road and continue north on the trail.

0.6   Reach a picnic area to the west. The trail turns sharply right (east).

0.8   Come to the Pittsburg Beach area. Continue hiking east across the park road and quickly approach the red connector trail that heads south. Continue hiking straight (east).

1.4   Reach a spur trail that leads to Indian Point. After checking out the scenery, return to the trail and continue hiking south on the Indian Point Trail.

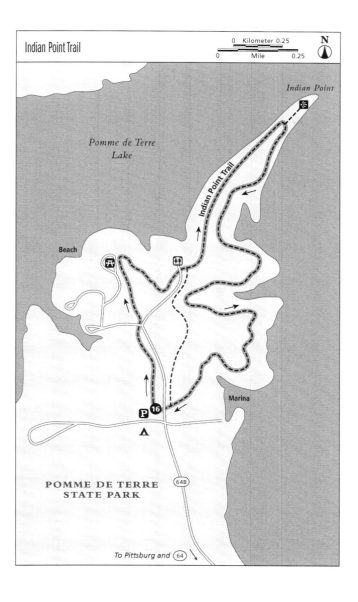

Indian Point Trail

Pomme de Terre Lake

Indian Point

Beach

Marina

P 16

POMME DE TERRE
STATE PARK

64B

To Pittsburg and 64

0   Kilometer   0.25
0   Mile   0.25

N

2.7 After hiking near the shore for a short stretch, come to a bench with a good view of the marina.

3.0 The red connector trail intersects from the north. Continue west on the Indian Point Trail and then cross the park road.

3.1 Arrive back at the trailhead.

17 Bennett Spring State Park: Savanna Ridge Trail

Hikers looking to escape the throngs that come to the park to fish will enjoy this getaway. After traveling past Bennett Spring and accessing the trail, you'll have the hardwood forest almost to yourself in this beautiful Ozark setting. The trail meanders gently through the forest for an enjoyable day hike.

Distance: 2.6-mile lollipop
Hiking time: About 1.5 hours
Difficulty: Moderate due to length
Best season: Fall through spring
Other trail users: None
Canine compatibility: Leashed dogs permitted
Fees and permits: No fees or permits required
Schedule: Trail is open from sunrise to sunset.

Maps: USGS Bennett Spring; trail guides available in the nature center and trailhead
Trail contacts: Bennett Spring State Park, 26250 MO 64A, Lebanon 65536; (417) 532-4338, www.bennettspringstate park.com
Special considerations: Ticks are common in warmer months. Trail may be inaccessible after heavy rainfall.

Finding the trailhead: From Lebanon drive (northwest) on MO 64 for 10.9 miles to MO 64A and the park entrance. Turn left (west) onto MO 64A and drive 0.9 mile to Bennett Spring State Park 7. Turn left onto BSSP 7; drive 0.1 mile before bearing left onto BSSP 2 and continuing another 0.2 mile. Bear right onto BSSP 3 and drive 0.1 mile to the parking area. GPS: N37 42.937' / W92 51.248'

The Hike

Bennett Spring State Park is home of the fourth-largest spring in the state of Missouri. James Brice built the first gristmill here in 1846, but his son-in-law Peter Bennett enjoyed the most success with it. The spring and state park were eventually named for the Bennett Family.

In 1900 that Missouri fish commissioner introduced 40,000 mountain trout into the spring to satisfy the growing number of recreationists and fishermen coming to the area. In 1923 a private fish hatchery was built, and in 1924 the state purchased the spring and part of the land to create one of Missouri's first state parks.

Although it's immensely popular with trout anglers, the 3,200-acre park offers much, much more than just fishing opportunities. Visitors can camp in either basic or improved campsites, go swimming in the pool, pick up supplies at the park store, rent canoes to go floating on the Niangua River, or see what is happening at the nature center. Of course there are hiking opportunities as well.

Hikers can make their way over to Spring Hollow to explore the park's backcountry. The 7.5-mile Natural Tunnel Trail is highlighted by the Bennett Spring Natural Tunnel—a collapsed cave that is 15 feet high, 50 feet wide, and 100 yards long. The Savanna Ridge Trail sets out from the same trailhead and offers similar views of the spring branches, bluff tops, hardwood forests, and classic Ozark streams.

The trailhead for the Savanna Ridge and Natural Tunnel Trails is located at the southern end of the parking area. The trails share the same trailhead and begin in the same hiking direction.

From the trailhead kiosk hike northwest along the dirt path, following the green arrows that mark the Savanna Ridge Trail. After 0.1 mile reach a service road; turn left (south) onto the road. Follow the road for only 0.1 mile before turning left (east) again to continue on the now grassy Savanna Ridge/Natural Tunnel Trail. At 0.3 mile reach the beginning of the loop portion of the hike. Turn right (south) onto the Savanna Ridge Trail and leave the Natural Tunnel Trail for a short while. The trails will reconnect to return to the trailhead later in the hike.

Continue hiking through the hardwood forest south until you come to the white-blazed connector trail, which breaks off to the east. Hikers looking for a shorter trek can take this route for a 1.5-miles round-trip.

Continue hiking south past the connector. At 1.3 miles the trail begins to descend the Savanna Ridge. Don't forget your fern identification card so that you can identify some of the beautiful ferns that line the trail during this section.

Around 1.6 miles reach the east end of the white connector trail; continue hiking to the right (northeast). In another 0.2 mile (1.8 miles) the Savanna Ridge Trail reconnects with the Natural Tunnel Trail. Hikers looking to extend their trip can turn south here.

Turn left (north) to complete the Savanna Ridge Trail loop. After turning left (north), hike along the bottom until the loop portion of the hike ends at 2.2 miles. Continue hiking straight (west) to return to the trailhead at 2.6 miles.

Miles and Directions

0.0   Start at the Natural Tunnel/Savanna Ridge Trailhead and begin following the obvious dirt path northwest into the woodlands.

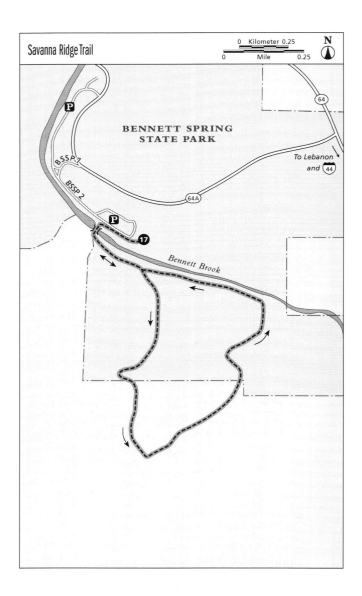

Savanna Ridge Trail

0   Kilometer   0.25

0   Mile   0.25

N

BENNETT SPRING
STATE PARK

P

BSSP 7

BSSP 2

P

64A

64

To Lebanon
and 44

17

Bennett Brook

0.1   Turn left (south) onto a service road and cross a bridge before heading up hill.

0.2   Leave the service road, turning left (southeast) onto the well-marked Savanna Ridge Trail (green arrows).

0.3   Come to the beginning of the loop; turn right (south) to continue on the Savanna Ridge Trail.

0.8   Intersect the white connector trail. Stay right (south) on the Savanna Ridge Trail. (**Option:** Bear left (east) onto the connector trail for a 1.5-mile hike.)

1.3   The trail continues down the ridge and passes several ferns and a buckeye tree that may already be turning fall colors as early as July.

1.6   Reach the east end of the white connector trail; continue right (northeast) on the Savanna Ridge Trail.

1.8   The Savanna Ridge Trail rejoins the Natural Tunnel Trail. Stay left (north).

2.2   Reach the end of the loop. Turn right (west) to return to the trailhead.

2.6   Arrive back at the trailhead.

18 Ha Ha Tonka State Park: Devil's Kitchen Trail

A short hike through a state park well known for its numerous hiking trails, the Devil's Kitchen Trail packs many of the park's tourist sites into one hike. A large sinkhole, glades, chert woodlands, a natural bridge, and views of the old castle ruins are just some of the wonders this trek has to offer.

Distance: 1.4-mile loop
Hiking time: About 1.5 hours
Difficulty: Moderate due to rocky trails and climb
Best season: Fall through spring
Other trail users: None
Canine compatibility: Leashed dogs permitted
Fees and permits: No fees or permits required
Schedule: Park open 7 a.m. to sunset Apr through Oct; 8 a.m. to sunset Nov through Mar

Maps: USGS Hahatonka; trail and natural area guides available in the visitor center
Trail contacts: Ha Ha Tonka State Park, 1491 State Road D, Camdenton 65020; (573) 346-2986; http://mostateparks.com/park/ha-ha-tonka-state-park
Special considerations: Ticks are common in warmer months.

Finding the trailhead: From Camdenton drive southwest on US 54 W for 2.4 miles. Turn left (south) onto State Road D and drive 2.2 miles to the Devil's Kitchen trailhead parking area on the left (east). GPS: N37 58.423' / W92 45.749'

The Hike

The area that is now Ha Ha Tonka State Park was almost Missouri's first state park. Governor Herbert Hadley proposed the idea in 1909, but it was rejected. Ha Ha Tonka didn't become a state park until 1978—surprising when you consider that this area is known as "Missouri's karst showcase."

Features like a 70-foot-wide and 60-foot-long natural bridge, 150-foot-deep sinkholes, numerous caves, and even old castle ruins would seem to make this area a shoe-in for a state park. In 1903 Robert Snyder was so impressed with the area that he purchased over 5,000 acres here to build a European style castle as a retreat. Snyder began building his elaborate getaway in 1905 but was killed in one of the country's first automobile accidents only a year later. His sons finished the work, and the castle functioned as a hotel until 1942, when it was accidentally burned to the ground.

Hikers on the Devil's Kitchen Trail get a few glimpses of the old castle ruins and have the option to visit the ruins via connecting trails. The 1.4-mile loop also passes some of the most amazing natural features the park has to offer. The park that was carved from stone will have you wanting more after you hike the Devil's Kitchen Trail.

From the trailhead parking area, begin hiking south on the gravel trail. The trail slowly rises up a moderate slope and quickly intersects Acorn Trail at 0.1 mile. Stay to the right and continue hiking south, following the brown blazes for the Devil's Kitchen Trail. The trail continues through an open woodland savanna and begins going downhill, reaching the Devil's Kitchen and Promenade at 0.4 mile.

Continue hiking through Devil's Kitchen and make your way up and across a large opening in the rocks. Step across the gap, make your way along the ledge that circles the sinkhole, and eventually begin climbing out of the Kitchen. At 0.7 mile, cross over Post Office Road and continue hiking northwest until you reach the Post Office Shelter Area at

0.9 mile. Turn right (north) to follow the footprints across State Road D into the Spring Trail parking area, and proceed down the stairs where the Devil's Kitchen Trail and Spring Trail join each other briefly. At the bottom of the stairs turn right (east) and continue to 1.1 miles to where the Spring Trail splits away to the left (northwest) and the Devil's Kitchen Trail continues northeast.

At 1.2 miles turn right (northeast) to continue following the brown blazes. Shortly thereafter take a sharp right (southeast) at a picnic area to cross over the natural bridge. The Colosseum sinkhole will be to your left and right as you cross over the bridge. At 1.4 miles cross over State Road D again and return to the trailhead parking area.

Miles and Directions

0.0 Start at the trailhead kiosk and turn left (south) onto the gravel trail, heading up a moderate slope.

0.1 Acorn Trail splits to the left; stay right (south) on the Devil's Kitchen Trail, following the brown blazes.

0.4 After descending a hill into the Devil's Kitchen and Promenade, continue past a cave and take a big step across an opening in the rocks before walking along a ledge above the sinkhole.

0.7 Cross Post Office Road to continue on the Devil's Kitchen Trail.

0.9 Turn right (north) at the Post Office Shelter area and follow the footprints across State Road D to continue down a set of stairs on the Devil's Kitchen Trail/Spring Trail.

1.0 At the bottom of the stairs, bear right (east) to stay on the Devil's Kitchen Trail.

1.1 The Spring Trail splits to the left (northwest); continue northeast on the Devil's Kitchen Trail.

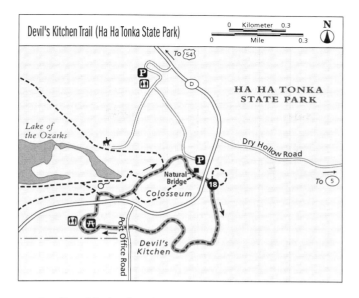

Devil's Kitchen Trail (Ha Ha Tonka State Park)

HA HA TONKA STATE PARK

Lake of the Ozarks

Dry Hollow Road

To 54

To 5

Natural Bridge

Colosseum

Devil's Kitchen

Post Office Road

18

1.2 Turn right (northeast) and continue following the brown blazes. Soon take another sharp right (southeast) to cross over the natural bridge.

1.4 Cross State Road D and arrive back at the trailhead parking area.

19 Lake of the Ozarks State Park: Lakeview Bend Trail

The Lake of the Ozarks is a popular destination for Missourians during summer and on long holiday weekends. Missouri's largest state park, Lake of the Ozarks sits just south of Osage Beach. The park covers more than 17,000 acres and contains twelve hiking trails.

Distance: 1.5-mile loop
Hiking time: About 1 to 1.5 hours
Difficulty: Moderate due to length
Best season: Year-round
Other trail users: None
Canine compatibility: Leashed dogs permitted
Fees and permits: No fees or permits required

Maps: USGS Lake Ozark; trail map available at visitor center
Trail contacts: Lake of the Ozarks State Park, 403 MO 134, Kaiser 65047; (573) 348-2694; http://mostateparks.com/park/lake-ozarks-state-park
Special considerations: Ticks and mosquitoes are common during warmer months.

Finding the trailhead: From Osage Beach drive south on MO 134/MO 42. After 3.5 miles turn right (south) to stay on MO 134 east. Continue 4.7 miles into the Lake of the Ozarks State Park. Trailhead parking is located at the campground entrance. GPS: N38 4.572' / W92 34.239'

The Hike

The largest state park in Missouri, Lake of the Ozarks covers more than 17,000 acres in the Ozark Highlands. Originally established by the National Park Service in the 1930s, the park was turned over to Missouri State Parks in 1946. The park is on the National Register of Historic Place due to the old bridges, log cabins, and Civilian Conservation Corps buildings within the park.

The park offers many recreational opportunities. Chert woodlands, springs, caves, and of course the lakes are just a few of the natural highlights in the park. Explorers can tour caves that are highlighted by bear claw marks, bats, and a feature called Angels' Showers. The waterfall-like showers seem to pour right out of the rocks in an endless stream.

Water sports enthusiasts will find no shortage here. Facilities include two beaches for swimming, two marinas for boating, and boat rentals. The park also has plenty of options for hikers on its twelve trails. Some trails are as short as 0.8 mile, others as long as 13.5 miles. At 1.5 miles the Lakeview Bend Trail is on the shorter side, but it offers great views of the water.

The Lakeview Bend Trailhead is located east of the campground registration booth. Begin hiking southeast down the rocky trail. At just 0.1-mile the trail turns right (south) and traverses a steep rocky ridge that rises high above the lakeshore below. Continue hiking through the oak and hickory forest in a southwest direction before descending to the lakeshore at 0.7-mile. Turning right (northwest) here, the trail climbs uphill away from the lakeshore and enters a more populated area as it passes through the campground. The trail crosses the campground road at 0.8 mile and passes several places that are ideal for picnics or for a short stop at a playground.

At about 1.0-mile the trail leaves the campground and returns to a more wooded area. The trail continues through

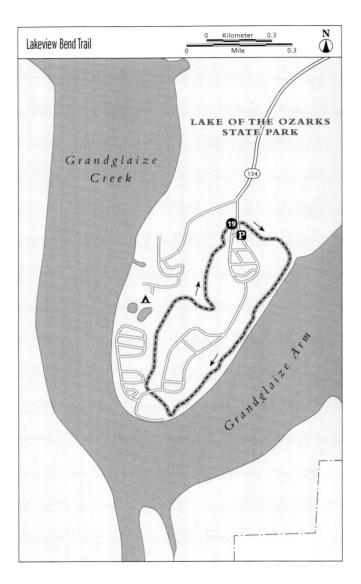

Kilometer

Mile

N

LAKE OF THE OZARKS
STATE PARK

134

*Grandglaize
Creek*

19

P

Grandglaize Arm

the woodland and reaches a sharp left (north) turn at 1.2 miles. Right after the turn, cross a footbridge and continue north up a gradual hill. Reach the end of the loop and the small parking area just outside the campground registration booth at 1.5 miles.

Miles and Directions

0.0 Start on the trail to the east of the campground registration building and begin hiking clockwise (southeast).

0.1 Turn right (south) and follow the trail along the steep rocky terrain above the shoreline.

0.7 The trail dips to the lakeshore and turns right (northwest) before climbing uphill.

0.8 Cross the campground road and continue hiking northwest.

1.0 Leave the campground and return to a more wooded area.

1.2 The trail makes a sharp left (north) turn and crosses a footbridge.

1.5 Arrive back at the trailhead.

20 Clifty Creek Natural and Conservation Areas: Clifty Creek Trail

Clifty Creek Trail offers a trip through a beautiful natural area and a conservation area in the same hike. The journey to the 40-foot-long natural bridge affords a chance to see some of the 450 plant species that have been recorded in the area.

Distance: 2.5-mile loop
Hiking time: About 2 to 2.5 hours
Difficulty: More challenging due to terrain
Best season: Year-round
Other trail users: None
Canine compatibility: Leashed dogs permitted
Fees and permits: No fees or permits required
Maps: USGS Nagogami Lodge; trail map available at trailhead

Trail contacts: MDC Central Regional Office, 1907 Hillcrest Dr., Columbia 65201; (573) 882-8388; http://mdc4 .mdc.mo.gov/applications/ moatlas/AreaSummaryPage .aspx?txtAreaID=7309
Special considerations: Sturdy footwear should be worn on this trail. A creek crossing is required to complete the loop.

Finding the trailhead: From Dixon drive 3.7 miles on MO 28 east. Turn right (east) onto State Road W and continue for 3.4 miles to where the pavement ends. The road becomes gravel and is now CR 511. Drive 1 mile on CR 511 to the parking area on the left (north) side of the road. GPS: N38 1.837' / W91 58.912'

The Hike

Clifty Creek became Missouri's first designated natural area in 1971. With the addition of the Clifty Creek Conservation Area in the 1980s, the combined areas now comprise 486 acres of scenic dolomite cliffs. Hikers here can expect to see a typical Missouri Ozarks hardwood forest filled with northern red oaks, white oaks, and mockernut hickories. Clifty Creek is also a popular spot for birders and animal lovers. Deer, squirrel, and turkey can be seen in the area and with permits can be hunted during hunting season. The only trail in the area takes hikers on a beautiful and scenic tour over some of the best the land has to offer.

Locate the trailhead at the northeast corner of the parking lot and start hiking counterclockwise (west). After just 0.1 mile turn right to begin the loop portion of the trail; begin a slow descent into Clifty Hollow. The trail continues a series of ups and downs until you reach the bottom of the hollow and Clifty Creek. At 1.0 mile reach Clifty Creek and the Clifty Creek Natural Bridge. You will need to cross the creek here to continue the loop. Hikers who are not prepared to get their feet wet can simply turn around and return to the trailhead via the same route they just descended.

After crossing Clifty Creek, look for where the trail continues on the left (west) side of the natural bridge without going under it. Continue hiking up and out of the hollow. At 1.3 miles reach the top of the hollow and hike southwest along the rocky ridgeline as it parallels Clifty Creek and Clifty Hollow.

The trail descends back down into the hollow at 2.2 miles and then crosses Clifty Creek again before climbing

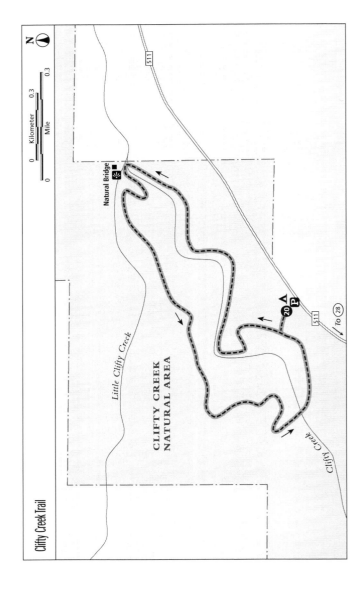

Clifty Creek Trail

out of the hollow one more time toward the southeast. Reach the end of the loop portion of the hike at 2.4 miles; turn right (east) to return to the trailhead.

Miles and Directions

0.0   Start at the trailhead and begin hiking west .

0.1   Turn right (north) onto the loop portion of the trail and begin descending into Clifty Hollow.

1.0   Reach Clifty Creek Natural Bridge. Cross Clifty Creek and locate the trail to the left (west) of the bridge. Continue hiking southwest on the trail. (**Option:** If you don't want to get your feet wet, turn around at the creek and retrace your route to the trailhead.)

1.3   Reach the north ridge of Clifty Hollow and continue southwest.

2.2   Trail descends back down in Clifty Hollow and crosses Clifty Creek again.

2.4   Reach the end of loop; turn right.

2.5   Arrive back at the trailhead.

About the Authors

JD Tanner grew up playing and exploring in the hills of southern Illinois. He has earned a degree in Outdoor Recreation from Southeast Missouri State University and an advanced degree in Outdoor Recreation from Southern Illinois University in Carbondale. He has traveled extensively throughout the United States and is the coordinator for outdoor recreation at San Juan College.

Emily Ressler-Tanner grew up in southeastern Missouri and southeastern Idaho. She spent her early years fishing, hiking, and camping with her family. In college she enjoyed trying out many new outdoor activities, graduating from Southern Illinois University with an advanced degree in Recreation Resource Administration.

Together they have climbed, hiked, paddled, and camped all over the United States. They coinstructed college-level outdoor recreation courses for several years before joining the staff at the Leave No Trace Center for Outdoor Ethics as traveling trainers. They have written revisions for two books for FalconGuides, *Best Easy Day Hikes Grand Staircase–Escalante* and *Hiking Grand Staircase–Escalante,* and coauthored *Best Easy Day Hikes Springfield, Missouri; Best Easy Day Hikes St. Louis; and Best Hikes Near St. Louis.* They currently reside in northwestern New Mexico.

WHAT'S SO SPECIAL ABOUT UNSPOILED, NATURAL PLACES?

Beauty Solitude Wildness Freedom Quiet Adventure
Serenity Inspiration Wonder Excitement
Relaxation Challenge

There's a lot to love about our treasured public lands, and the reasons are different for each of us. Whatever your reasons are, the national **Leave No Trace** education program will help you discover special outdoor places, enjoy them, and preserve them—today and for those who follow. By practicing and passing along these simple principles, you can help protect the special places you love from being loved to death.

THE PRINCIPLES OF **LEAVE NO TRACE**

- 🍂 Plan ahead and prepare
- 🍂 Travel and camp on durable surfaces
- 🍂 Dispose of waste properly
- 🍂 Leave what you find
- 🍂 Minimize campfire impacts
- 🍂 Respect wildlife
- 🍂 Be considerate of other visitors

Leave No Trace is a national nonprofit organization dedicated to teaching responsible outdoor recreation skills and ethics to everyone who enjoys spending time outdoors.

To learn more or to become a member, please visit us at www.LNT.org or call (800) 332-4100.

Leave No Trace, P.O. Box 997, Boulder, CO 80306

AMERICAN HIKING SOCIETY

Because you
hike.
We're with you
every step of the way

American Hiking Society gives voice to the more than 75 million Americans who hike and is the only national organization that promotes and protects foot trails, the natural areas that surround them, and the hiking experience. Our work is inspiring and challenging, and is built on three pillars:

Volunteerism and Stewardship
We organize and coordinate nationally recognized programs—including Volunteer Vacations, National Trails Day ®, and the National Trails Fund—that help keep our trails open, safe, and enjoyable.

Policy and Advocacy
We work with Congress and federal agencies to ensure funding for trails, the preservation of natural areas, and the protection of the hiking experience.

Outreach and Education
We expand and support the national constituency of hikers through outreach and education as well as partnerships with other recreation and conservation organizations.

Join us in our efforts. Become an American Hiking Society member today!

American Hiking Society

1422 Fenwick Lane · Silver Spring, MD 20910 · (800) 972-8608
www.AmericanHiking.org · info@AmericanHiking.org